ADHD

by Andrea C. Nakaya

Diseases and Disorders

ReferencePoint
Press™

San Diego, CA

© 2009 ReferencePoint Press, Inc.

For more information, contact:
ReferencePoint Press, Inc.
PO Box 27779
San Diego, CA 92198
www. ReferencePointPress.com

Picture credits:
Maury Aaseng: 32–34, 47–50, 65–68, 82–85
AP Images: 15
Landov: 17

Nakaya, Andrea C., 1976–
    Adhd / by Andrea C. Nakaya.
        p. cm.—(Compact research)
    Includes bibliographical references and index.
    ISBN-13: 978-1-60152-062-3 (hardback)
    ISBN-10: 1-60152-062-X (hardback)
    1. Attention-deficit hyperactivity disorder. I. Title.
    RJ506.H9N348 2008
    618.92'8589—dc22
                                                              2008031540

Contents

Foreword

As modern civilization continues to evolve, its ability to create, store, distribute, and access information expands exponentially. The explosion of information from all media continues to increase at a phenomenal rate. By 2020 some experts predict the worldwide information base will double every 73 days. While access to diverse sources of information and perspectives is paramount to any democratic society, information alone cannot help people gain knowledge and understanding. Information must be organized and presented clearly and succinctly in order to be understood. The challenge in the digital age becomes not the creation of information, but how best to sort, organize, enhance, and present information.

ReferencePoint Press developed the *Compact Research* series with this challenge of the information age in mind. More than any other subject area today, researching current issues can yield vast, diverse, and unqualified information that can be intimidating and overwhelming for even the most advanced and motivated researcher. The *Compact Research* series offers a compact, relevant, intelligent, and conveniently organized collection of information covering a variety of current topics ranging from illegal immigration and methamphetamine to diseases such as anorexia and meningitis.

The series focuses on three types of information: objective single-author narratives, opinion-based primary source quotations, and facts and statistics. The clearly written objective narratives provide context and reliable background information. Primary source quotes are carefully selected and cited, exposing the reader to differing points of view. And facts and statistics sections aid the reader in evaluating perspectives. Presenting these key types of information creates a richer, more balanced learning experience.

For better understanding and convenience, the series enhances information by organizing it into narrower topics and adding design features that make it easy for a reader to identify desired content. For example, in *Compact Research: Illegal Immigration*, a chapter covering the economic impact of illegal immigration has an objective narrative explaining the various ways the economy is impacted, a balanced section of numerous primary source quotes on the topic, followed by facts and full-color illustrations to encourage evaluation of contrasting perspectives.

The ancient Roman philosopher Lucius Annaeus Seneca wrote, "It is quality rather than quantity that matters." More than just a collection of content, the *Compact Research* series is simply committed to creating, finding, organizing, and presenting the most relevant and appropriate amount of information on a current topic in a user-friendly style that invites, intrigues, and fosters understanding.

ADHD at a Glance

Prevalence

While estimates vary, the prevalence of ADHD is estimated at between 3 and 10 percent worldwide. It is more common in youth and in males.

Causes

The causes of ADHD are unknown, and theories about them are controversial. However, most people believe ADHD is related to brain structure and chemistry and that genetics plays a role. The role that diet, parenting, and environmental toxins play in ADHD is more controversial.

Subjectivity of Diagnosis

ADHD cannot be definitively tested, and so some people charge that it is not a valid medical disorder.

Increasing Diagnosis Rates

Increased diagnosis rates have caused controversy; some people believe that the disorder is overdiagnosed, while others argue that awareness of ADHD has simply increased.

Effects on Daily Life

While some people maintain that those with ADHD can benefit from their differences, most people believe that ADHD has a negative impact on both individuals and society.

ADHD in Adults

It is estimated that two out of three children with ADHD continue to have problems with the disorder into adulthood. As awareness of ADHD grows, an increasing number of adults are being diagnosed and medicated for it.

Drug Treatment

Stimulants and other medications are the most common treatment for ADHD, but they are controversial because of their potential side effects.

Alternatives to Medication

Alternatives to ADHD drugs include education and therapy, special diets, and biofeedback; however, effectiveness of these treatments remains unproved.

Abuse of ADHD Medication

As diagnosis rates have increased, so has abuse of ADHD medication; numerous studies show that a significant number of youth have used stimulants nonmedically.

Overview

In the first half of the twentieth century, attention deficit hyperactivity disorder (ADHD) was rarely diagnosed and almost never treated with medication. Today, the American Psychiatric Association estimates that 3 to 7 percent of children in the United States have the disorder, and research shows that millions of them are taking medication. ADHD has become an important public health concern in the United States and around the world. It is very well researched, yet it remains extremely controversial. Researchers, policy makers, and the general public continue to offer varying opinions on what causes ADHD, how it affects a person's life, and how it should be treated.

What Is ADHD?

Attention Deficit Hyperactivity Disorder (ADHD) is a condition that affects both children and adults and is characterized by problems with attention, impulsivity, and hyperactivity. According to the American Psychiatric Association's *Diagnostic and Statistical Manual,* used by mental health professionals in diagnosing ADHD, these problems must be present at higher than normal levels and must interfere with a person's ability to function in different settings, such as home and school. The behaviors must appear before age seven and continue for at least six months. ADHD cannot be cured. Instead, treatment focuses on managing the symptoms.

> " [ADHD] is very well researched, yet it remains extremely controversial. "

ADHD has three subtypes: People with Predominantly Inattentive Type often have difficulty paying attention to details, finishing tasks, and are easily distracted or forgetful. Those with Predominantly Hyperactive-Impulsive Type fidget and talk a lot, move excessively or feel restless, interrupt others or speak at inappropriate times, and have difficulty waiting their turn. People with Combined Type have a combination of the inattentive and hyperactive-impulsive symptoms.

While the disorder has been recognized as far back in time as the 1800s, in 1980 it was officially named Attention Deficit Disorder (ADD) by the American Psychiatric Association (APA). In 1987 the term was changed to ADHD to show that hyperactivity is an important element. A person does not need to be hyperactive to be diagnosed with ADHD; however, some people continue to use the term ADD to refer to people that do not show hyperactivity. Others use the two terms interchangeably. However, the official term is ADHD.

How Common Is ADHD?

Estimates on the prevalence of ADHD vary widely. In the United States, the APA reports that 3 to 7 percent of children have the disorder. By most assessments, it is approximately three times more common in boys than in girls. While estimates on the rate among adults are less precise, various researchers maintain that anywhere from one-third to two-thirds of children who have the disorder will continue to have problems with it as adults. While ADHD rates appear to be highest in the United States, research reveals that the disorder is also common around the world. In a

2006 study published in the *European Journal of Pediatrics*, Maria Skounti, Anastas Philalithis, and Emmanouil Galanakis review all the studies in *PubMed*—an online database that includes millions of biomedical articles—between 1992 and 2005. These studies, from countries all over the world, indicate ADHD prevalence rates ranging from 4 to 10 percent. Not only is ADHD very common worldwide, but rates of ADHD have increased significantly in recent years. According to 2008 testimony by Nora D. Volkow, director of the National Institute on Drug Abuse (NIDA), in the United States the total number of stimulant prescriptions—the most common treatment for ADHD—increased from 5 million in 1991 to almost 35 million in 2007.

What Causes ADHD?

No one knows exactly what causes ADHD, but extensive research on the disorder points to numerous possibilities, some biological and some environmental. Most researchers believe ADHD is related to brain structure and chemistry, which appear to differ in people with the disorder. However, the reason for the differences is unclear. In addition, studies show that ADHD is heritable, providing strong evidence that genetics also plays a role. Recent research also shows that in some cases the disorder may be a result of slower maturation of some parts of the brain. Finally, there is evidence that ADHD might be caused by diet, gender, exposure to environmental toxins, or even the way a child is raised. In light of such a variety of potential causes, and because cases of ADHD differ so much between people, many experts believe there is no single cause of ADHD. Richard D. Rodd, professor of psychiatry and of genetics at the Washington University School of Medicine in St. Louis explains by comparing ADHD to diabetes, another common health problem. He says: "There can be lots of reasons why you become diabetic. . . . The end result is high blood sugar . . . but how that happens can differ greatly from individual to individual. It's the same thing for ADHD."[1]

According to the Centers for Disease Control and Prevention's

> " [ADHD] is approximately three times more common in boys than in girls. "

(CDC) National Center on Birth Defects and Developmental Disabilities, as many as half of those with ADHD have other mental disorders as well. For example, researchers estimate that almost half of children with ADHD have oppositional defiant disorder, which results in hostile and defiant behavior. Conduct disorder is also common, and results in aggression toward people or animals, and destruction of property. In addition, ADHD can be correlated with Tourette's syndrome, a disorder characterized by physical and vocal tics. Tourette's affects only a small percentage of those with ADHD, but according to the National Alliance on Mental Illness, at least half of those with Tourette's have ADHD. In addition to other mental disorders, people with ADHD often have learning disabilities such as dyslexia. The National Institute of Mental Health (NIMH) estimates that approximately 20 to 30 percent of children with ADHD also have a specific learning disability.

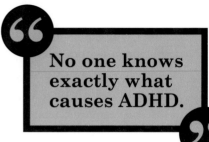

No one knows exactly what causes ADHD.

Because ADHD often coexists with other disorders and disabilities, misdiagnosis is very common. In the opinion of researchers Nadia Webb and Antara Dietrich, "Attention Deficit Disorders are the 'poster children' for the problem of misidentification and misdiagnosis."[2] When a person has both ADHD and another mental disorder or learning disability, medical professionals often have difficulty diagnosing exactly what the patient is suffering from. In addition, the symptoms of ADHD can be similar to some other conditions such as depression, anxiety, or bipolar disorder, making it even more difficult to accurately diagnose.

Subjectivity of ADHD Diagnosis

Doctors have no blood test, brain scan, or any kind of definitive test they can use to determine whether a person has ADHD. Instead, this disorder is diagnosed based on behavioral observation. For example, doctors look for things such as whether a person talks excessively, is easily distracted, or has difficulty following instructions. Whether these behaviors are seen as problematic and as symptoms of ADHD can depend a lot on the observer and what he or she believes is developmentally and culturally appropriate. Thus, a diagnosis of ADHD is extremely subjective.

Because of the subjectivity of an ADHD diagnosis, some people charge that it is not a real disorder, just a convenient explanation for problematic behavior. In the ADHD literature, many critics argue that society does not have enough tolerance for youth who exhibit problematic behavior. They maintain that instead, the trend is to label these children with an ADHD diagnosis and treat them with drugs. Fred A. Baughman Jr., a child neurologist, insists that no evidence that ADHD is a disease has been found. He says, "I have discovered and described real diseases and, having examined hundreds said to have this 'disorder' or 'disease,' I have found nothing wrong, abnormal or diseased about them. . . . It is the biggest health care fraud in history."[3] The subjectivity of an ADHD diagnosis in children is even more pronounced than in adults. Explains journalist Melissa Healy, "The boundary between troublesome behavior and mental illness is indistinct in adults, psychiatrists acknowledge; in children, whose brains are still a work in progress, it is fuzzier still."[4]

Effects on Life

Most people believe that ADHD has a harmful impact on an individual's life. Brian B. Doyle, professor of psychiatry at Georgetown University in Washington, D.C., says, "Many . . . have diminished life prospects and are subject to anxiety, affective disorders, and substance abuse. Many fail to reach their potential. There is a high cost in human suffering as well as in lost productivity."[5] The overall negative effect of ADHD is also described by the American Academy of Child and Adolescent Psychiatry. It says, "Untreated ADHD can have lifetime consequences. Compared with the general population, individuals with untreated ADHD have higher rates of divorce and job loss. They also have higher rates of cigarette and drug addiction, and more driving infractions."[6]

> " Recent research . . . shows that in some cases the disorder may be a result of slower maturation of some parts of the brain. "

However, some people insist that the excitement and energy that often come with ADHD can be beneficial if an individual learns how to utilize these strengths and manage the negative characteristics of the disorder. Says Doyle, "Some resourceful, talented individuals who have the disorder live successfully and creatively."[7] One successful individual who has been diagnosed with ADHD is David Neeleman, founder of JetBlue Airlines. He credits his success with his ADHD-related ability to focus on new ideas. "If you're doing something you love," says Neeleman, "you'll be the best."[8]

Drug Treatment

The most common treatment for ADHD is medication, and the most common class of medication used is stimulants. These include methylphenidate, with brand names Concerta, Metadate, Methylin, and Ritalin; amphetamine, Adderall; dextroamphetamine, Dexedrine and Dextrostat; and dexmethylphenidate, Focalin. These drugs work by affecting chemicals in the brain called neurotransmitters. Even though it seems counterintuitive that stimulants will help people who already seem to be overstimulated, these medications do help both adults and children focus and become less impulsive. There are short-acting versions that last about four hours, or long-acting versions that are taken only once or twice a day. The most common side effects from stimulants are decreased appetite, insomnia, nervousness, headache, and rapid heart rate. Another common ADHD medication is Strattera, a nonstimulant with the generic name atomoxetine. It can cause decreased appetite, upset stomach, nausea, dizziness, fatigue, and mood swings. This drug has also caused some cases of liver failure. In addition to stimulants and Strattera, doctors sometimes prescribe other drugs, including antidepressants, antihypertensives, and antipsychotics, which are not approved by the U.S. Food and Drug Administration for treating ADHD but have been found to help control ADHD symptoms in some people.

> " Because ADHD often coexists with other disorders and disabilities, misdiagnosis is very common. "

Treating ADHD with medication is controversial. In a 2005 report on ADHD prevalence and treatment in the United States, the CDC cautions, "Persistent and negative side effects of stimulants have been documented, including sleep disturbances, reduced appetite, and suppressed growth, which might have important health implications for the millions of children who are currently taking medication for ADHD."[9] However, in an analysis of ADHD medication *Consumer Reports* argues that the risks of side effects are generally minimal. It says, "When people taking stimulants are closely monitored by doctors, use of the drugs is generally considered to be very safe. Under 5% of children have side effects that require them to stop taking a stimulant." However this organization also adds a caution, saying, "The long-term consequences of taking stimulants for years on end have not been fully evaluated in studies."[10]

Abuse of ADHD Drugs

As increasing numbers of people with ADHD take medication, non-medical use of ADHD drugs has also increased. In its 2006 report, the International Narcotics Control Board found that the level of abuse of prescription drugs, including stimulants prescribed for ADHD, is no less than abuse of illegal drugs such as ecstasy, cocaine, and heroin. According to a 2008 report by the Substance Abuse and Mental Health Services Administration, 2 percent of youth aged 12 to 17 used stimulants nonmedically in 2006. The increase among those aged 16 and 17 was 3.3 percent. In a 2005 article in the *Journal of American College Health* Kristina M. Hall et al. investigated the nonmedical use of stimulants at a Midwestern university. Of the 179 men surveyed, 17 percent reported illicit use of stimulants, as did 11 percent of the 202 women surveyed. Forty-four percent of students said they knew someone who engaged in illicit use of stimulants.

> **Most people believe that ADHD has a harmful impact on an individual's life.**

Research shows that much of the abuse of ADHD medication occurs among students. Many use it to help increase their cognitive function and academic performance in school. In congressional testimony Volkow stated, "In fact, being in college may even be a risk factor for greater use of amphetamines or Ritalin nonmedically."[11] Another factor contributing to increasing abuse of ADHD medication may be the increase of legitimate prescriptions, which makes it easier to obtain medication for nonmedical use. In addition, the prevalence of use contributes to the belief that ADHD medication is harmless for use without a prescription.

This pharmacist holds a bottle of Ritalin and a pamphlet warning parents about its abuse. The most common treatment for ADHD is medication. Research shows that much of the abuse of ADHD medication occurs among students.

Alternatives to ADHD Medication

While medication is the most common treatment for ADHD, various alternatives exist. Most people agree that therapy and education about how to cope with the symptoms of ADHD can be useful both for those with the disorder, and those who interact with them. Other treatments that have provoked more skepticism include special diets and nutritional supplements, regular exercise, chiropractic adjustments, and biofeed-back, a technique that teaches people to change their brain wave patterns to ones that are more normal. While many people claim such alternatives are effective, research to prove this is lacking.

It is widely believed that drugs are the most effective ADHD treatment, however a recent study shows that this may not be true. The NIMH funded one of the most intensive studies on the effect of ADHD treatments. Called the Multimodal Treatment Study of Children with Attention Deficit Hyperactivity Disorder (MTA), it included 579 elementary school children. Researchers randomly assigned the children to four groups: medication only, behavioral treatment only, a combination of both, or routine community care. In the initial 14 months of the study, the combination treatment and the medication-only treatment produced the best results. However, at the three-year point, medication was not shown to be more effective than other approaches. According to James M. Swanson, coauthor of four papers written about the study results, "[After three years] all the kids looked better, but the ones taking the medication were no better [than the others]."[12] This study indicates that the most important thing is to receive some kind of treatment, but not necessarily medication.

> "Treating ADHD with medication is controversial."

Controversy Concerning Diagnosis Rates

Significant controversy remains over the fact that an increasing number of both children and adults are being diagnosed with ADHD. Critics argue that many of them do not actually have a medical disorder. Instead, they say, the diagnosis of ADHD serves as an easy way to deal with behavior that is problematic or different from the majority of the population. ADHD expert Thomas Armstrong says,

> ADD/ADHD is a popular diagnosis . . . because it serves as a neat way to explain the complexities of . . . life in America. Over the past few decades, our families have broken up, respect for authority has eroded, mass media has created a 'short-attention-span culture,' and stress levels have skyrocketed. With our children starting to act out under the strain, it's convenient to create a scientific-sounding term to label them with.[13]

This high school senior, who has been diagnosed with ADHD, takes a quiz in the teachers' lounge so she can concentrate. Most people with ADHD have problems focusing and concentrating on tasks.

However, others contend that rates have increased only because awareness of the disorder has increased. They also argue that ADHD is actually underdiagnosed in many populations.

Most people believe it is important to recognize and treat ADHD, or it will have a harmful effect on a person's life. However, others argue that diagnosing and medically treating ADHD just causes more problems. Sami Timimi, child and adolescent psychiatrist and author of *Pathological Child Psychiatry and the Medicalization of Childhood* explains, "We create unnecessary dependence on doctors, discouraging children and their families from engaging their own abilities to solve problems."[14]

Adults and ADHD

While ADHD is not listed as a diagnosis for adults in the *American Psychiatric Manual*, the disorder is common among adults as well as children. Mental Health America (MHA) finds that two out of three children with ADHD maintain some symptoms into adulthood. However, many experts believe ADHD is underdiagnosed in adults because many do not realize they might have the disorder, and it is often more difficult to diagnose, because the hyperactivity element often lessens. Says the NIMH, "Typically, adults with ADHD are unaware that they have this disorder—they often just feel that it's impossible to get organized, to stick to a job, to keep an appointment."[15] Not realizing that they might have ADHD can cause problems for adults with the disorder, because they often suffer problems as a result of ADHD symptoms, but do not understand why. MHA explains, "Many [adults with ADHD] have been labeled as 'having a bad attitude,' 'a slow learner,' 'lacking motivation,' 'immature,' 'lazy,' 'spacey,' or 'self-centered.' . . . Many have come to accept the unsubstantiated belief that they themselves are to blame for their problems."[16]

> **Research shows that much of the abuse of ADHD medication occurs among students.**

Cultural Differences

Cultural differences affect ADHD diagnosis rates, with rates differing across the United States and between the United States and other countries. However, the implications for this are debatable. Some people believe it proves that culture plays a significant role in the existence of ADHD. Professor at the Institute of Psychiatry at King's College London Eric Taylor says, "The rates of clinically diagnosed cases differ enormously between societies, indicating a powerful part played by culture in defining the concepts of disorder."[17] F. Gonzalez-Lima, professor at the University of Texas at Austin, agrees. He says, "The same behavior may be culturally constructed as normal or may lead to a diagnosis of a psychiatric disorder. Adults from different cultures have widely different degrees of tolerance for children's disruptive behavior and rough and tumble play that result in different rates of diagnosis of ADHD."[18]

Other researchers contend that ADHD can be found all over the world, proving that it is not just a disease created by certain cultures.

For example, researchers from the University of California at Berkeley analyzed the rate of ADHD medication use between 1993 and 2003 in numerous countries. Coauthor of the study Stephen Hinshaw says, "A common misconception is that ADHD only exists in the U.S. . . . Yet cross-cultural research has shown that ADHD exists in nearly any culture that has compulsory education. Clearly, ADHD . . . is not just a figment of American doctors' imagination."[19]

Critics continue to debate what causes ADHD, how it affects a person's life, how it should be treated, and whether society needs to change the way it approaches this disorder. As the U.S. Department of Education points out, the answers to such questions are vitally important to society. It says, "Hanging in the balance of heated debates over medication, diagnostic methods, and treatment options are children, adolescents, and adults who must manage the condition and lead productive lives on a daily basis."[20]

What Causes ADHD?

Because ADHD is so prevalent in society, the question of what causes it is important. However no clear answers exist. As *ADDitude* magazine states, "Attention deficit disorder . . . is one of the most researched areas in child and adolescent mental health. However, the precise cause of the disorder is still unknown."[21] Most people agree that the disorder is related to brain structure and chemistry. Strong evidence also points to genetics. Other possible causes of ADHD include: a developmental delay, diet, parenting style, gender, environmental toxins, and social attitudes.

Brain Structure and Chemistry

Numerous studies show that people with ADHD often have differences in the structure and chemistry of their brains, and this is believed to be one of the reasons for the disorder. In people with ADHD, research shows less activity and blood flow in areas that control activity and attention. In addition, brain scans show that people with ADHD sometimes have smaller brain volumes compared with those who do not have ADHD. ADHD is also linked to chemicals called neurotransmitters, which send messages between nerve cells in the brain. It is widely believed that the disorder is the result of these chemicals not being used properly. Stimulant medication, the most common treatment for ADHD, stimulates the brain to release greater amounts of neurotransmitters.

However, brain structure and chemistry do not completely explain the existence of this disorder. While research shows differences in the brains of people with ADHD, it is less clear why such differences exist. Researchers are investigating numerous potential causes, including genetics, diet, gender, and environmental toxins.

Research shows that in some cases ADHD may be a result of slower brain development in children. In 2007 the National Institute on Mental Health (NIMH)

> **While research shows differences in the brains of people with ADHD, it is less clear why such differences exist.**

revealed the results of a study of numerous scans of the brains of 446 youth, half with ADHD, and half without it. The scans show that in about half of the youth with ADHD, the brain matures normally but is delayed an average of three years in some regions. The delay is most prominent in the cortex, which controls thinking, attention, and planning; activities that are often difficult for people with ADHD. This theory that ADHD is a result of developmental delay explains the fact that some children seem to grow out of the disorder.

However, not all children grow out of ADHD. As Philip Shaw, lead author of the NIMH study cautions, "While a lot of people with ADHD do improve with age, as many as two-thirds still have symptoms of the disorder which persist into adulthood."[22] So researchers believe that while a developmental delay might explain some cases of ADHD, other factors also influence the development of this disorder.

Genetics

Most people believe that genetics plays some role in the development of ADHD. Numerous studies show that the disorder is heritable. According to the Attention Deficit Disorder Association (ADDA), if one person in a family has ADHD, a 25 to 30 percent chance exists that someone else in the family also has the disorder, compared with only a 4 to 6 percent chance in the general population. The association also reports that if an identical twin has ADHD, the chance is 50 percent that the other twin will have it. ADHD expert Russell A. Barkley believes genetics is the single biggest influence on whether an individual will develop ADHD.

> "Research shows that . . . ADHD may be a result of slower brain development in children.

He says, "There is little question that heredity/genetics makes the largest contribution to the expression of the disorder in the population. . . . [It] rivals that for the role of genetics in human height."[23] Brian B. Doyle, professor of psychiatry at Georgetown University in Washington, D.C., agrees. He says, "Genetic studies show that ADHD is strongly inherited. . . . Adoption studies show that nature (genetic inheritance) is much more important than nurture (parenting style) in determining ADHD."[24]

Others believe that while genetics plays a role in ADHD, environmental factors are more important. Says medical doctor Edward M. Hallowell, "Remember . . . that inheriting the genes that predispose toward this condition doesn't guarantee getting it. It is not ADD that is inherited, but rather the predisposition toward developing it."[25] He believes that while genes can make it more likely for a person to develop ADHD, the disorder does not occur without the influence of environmental factors. Gabor Maté, medical doctor and author of *Scattered Minds: A New Look at the Origins and Healing of Attention Deficit Disorder*, argues that environmental influence is extremely important because so much brain development occurs after birth. "Nerve cells and neurological circuits compete for survival in a process that has been called 'neural Darwinism,'" he says. "Those receiving the necessary stimulation are strengthened and become wired in, those that do not fail to develop and may even die. [Failure to get that stimulation may] predispose children to ADD because they directly affect the developing electrical circuits of the infant's brain."[26]

Diet

Whether sugar or certain food additives play a role in the development of ADHD is also hotly debated. Many people believe that diet can cause

ADHD or significantly worsen its symptoms. In a recent study, published in the September 2007 issue of the *Lancet*, researchers report on a study of the effects of food additives on 297 children—a group of 3-year-olds and a group of 8- and 9-year-olds. They observed that children who consumed drinks with artificial food colorings and sodium benzoate, a common food preservative, had significantly more hyperactive behavior. However, most support for the link between diet and ADHD is based on the personal observations of parents and caregivers who are adamant that if they eliminate sugar or certain food additives from the diet of a child with ADHD, they see dramatic improvements. The most well-known dietary approach to treating ADHD is the Feingold diet, begun in the 1970s by medical doctor Ben Feingold. The diet eliminates a number of artificial colors, flavors, and preservatives from the diet, and many people claim it significantly improves hyperactivity. Says one mother on an ADHD-focused Web site: "Feingold worked like a charm for my son. We began in kindergarten. The results we got within two weeks were amazing. His hyperactivity went way down, he started to sleep, he could focus and learn."[27]

However, others insist that evidence is lacking to back up the theory that diet causes ADHD or has a significant impact on its symptoms. According to the National Alliance on Mental Illness, "Scientific studies have not verified dietary factors . . . as a main cause of the disorder."[28] The NIMH also reports that in scientific studies, only a very small percentage of children show an improvement in ADHD symptoms as a result of dietary changes. In a review of the research on ADHD, researcher D. Daley agrees. He says, "While improving children's diet might impact on their general health and improve their overall behavior, the clinical importance of dietary change as a means of remediating ADHD remains doubtful."[29]

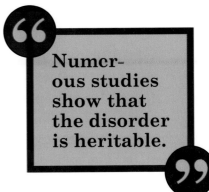

"Numerous studies show that the disorder is heritable.

Parenting

Some people believe that parenting style is an important factor in whether a child will develop ADHD. Most researchers agree that ADHD does have some biological basis, however these proponents believe that while a per-

> **Many people believe that diet can cause ADHD or significantly worsen its symptoms.**

son may be predisposed to the disorder, whether they actually develop it is also dependent on parenting. For example, according to Maté, "[The developing brains of young children] need the appropriate input: a calm, non-stressed connection with a non-stressed and non-distracted primary maternal caregiver. Stresses on the mothering adult—or disruption of contact with her . . . predispose children to ADD because they directly affect the developing . . . brain."[30]

Others insist that while parenting style can make ADHD symptoms better or worse, it is not caused by poor parenting. The NIMH says, "There is little compelling evidence at this time that ADHD can arise purely from social factors or child-rearing methods."[31] And the ADDA maintains, "ADHD is <u>NOT</u> caused by poor parenting. . . . ADHD <u>IS</u> very likely caused by biological factors."[32]

Gender

Because ADHD is approximately three times more common in boys than in girls, some people argue that simply being male increases a person's chance of developing the disorder. However others caution that ADHD diagnosis rates may not correctly reflect the actual number of cases of ADHD in boys versus girls. Child and adolescent psychiatrist Larry B. Silver argues that boys are more likely to be aggressive or antisocial as a result of the disorder and thus get noticed more than girls. He says, "Despite having attention problems similar to those of boys with ADHD, girls with ADHD are less intrusive and show fewer aggressive symptoms; thus, they are less likely to come to the attention of their teachers or other professionals."[33] Doyle points out that ADHD research and treatment has historically focused more on males than females. However, he says, "Many more [girls and women] have the disorder than we used to think."[34]

Environmental Toxins

Some people charge that ADHD is a result of exposure to environmental toxins, either before a child is born, or during childhood; both periods of time when the brain is developing rapidly and is susceptible to damage. There is evidence that the disorder can occur when the developing brain of a fetus is exposed to alcohol, tobacco or other drugs during pregnancy. In addition, some research shows a correlation between exposure to environmental toxins and rates of ADHD in children. Deborah Merlin, coauthor of *Victory over ADHD: How a Mother's Journey to Natural Medicine Reversed Her Children's Severe Emotional, Mental, and Behavioral Problems*, explains that environmental toxins can accumulate in the body and disrupt its normal function. She says, "Environmental toxins saturate our world. Our children come into frequent contact with mercury, lead, aluminum, pesticides and other toxins, such as fire retardants found in cars and electronic equipment." In her opinion, it is impossible to say that these toxins have no effect on health. She argues, "We are facing an epidemic of neurological and learning disorders that can't be explained away by simple genetics."[35]

The Role of Society

Some people believe that ADHD is not a real medical condition but something that has been created by society. Researchers Sami Timimi and Nick Radcliffe point out that no medical test for ADHD exists; instead it is based on opinion. They say, "Despite years and millions of dollars spent on research . . . no medical test for it exists, nor has any proof been forthcoming of what the supposed physical deficit is, and so diagnosis is based on the subjective opinion of the diagnoser. Indeed, its validity as a distinct diagnostic entity is widely questioned."[36] Timimi, Radcliffe, and others believe that ADHD came to be defined as a disorder because society wanted a medical explanation for behavior that is problematic or different from average. Says ADHD expert Thomas Armstrong, "Over the past few decades, our families have broken up, respect for authority has eroded, mass media has created a 'short-attention-span culture,' and stress levels have skyrocketed. When our children start to act out under the strain, it's convenient to create a scientific-sounding term to label them with."[37]

> " Some research shows a correlation between exposure to environmental toxins and rates of ADHD. "

However, others insist that while no medical test can diagnose ADHD, it is characterized by specific and observable behaviors, and can thus be medically diagnosed. According to the 2002 International Consensus Statement on ADHD, made by a group of leading scientists, researchers, and clinicians treating ADHD, "All of the major medical associations and government health agencies recognize ADHD as a genuine disorder because the scientific evidence is so overwhelming." They insist, "To publish stories that ADHD is a fictitious disorder . . . is tantamount to declaring the earth flat, the laws of gravity debatable."[38]

While ADHD may have a variety of possible causes, no cause is clear. However, as ADHD rates increase around the world, the question of what causes the disorder becomes more important. Researchers, policy makers, and the general public continue to investigate the links between ADHD and potential causes such as brain structure and chemistry, genetics, brain development, diet, parenting style, gender, environmental toxins, and social attitudes.

What Causes ADHD?

> **In this [study] . . . we tested the effects of artificial food additives on children's behavior and have shown that a mix of additives commonly found in children's food increases . . . hyperactivity in children aged 3 years and 8/9 years.**

—Donna McCann et al., "Food Additives and Hyperactive Behavior in 3-Year-Old and 8/9-Year-Old Children in the Community: A Randomised Double-Blinded, Placebo-Controlled Study," *Lancet*, September 6, 2007. www.thelancet.com.

The authors are all affiliated with the School of Psychology at the University of Southampton in the United Kingdom.

> **There is no proof that food additives cause attention-deficit/hyperactivity disorder.**

—Mayo Clinic, "ADHD Diet: Do Food Additives Cause Hyperactivity?" January 8, 2008. www.mayoclinic.com.

The Mayo Clinic is a nonprofit medical practice that also works to provide the public with reliable health information on a variety of topics, including ADHD.

Bracketed quotes indicate conflicting positions.

* Editor's Note: While the definition of a primary source can be narrowly or broadly defined, for the purposes of Compact Research, a primary source consists of: 1) results of original research presented by an organization or researcher; 2) eyewitness accounts of events, personal experience, or work experience; 3) first-person editorials offering pundits' opinions; 4) government officials presenting political plans and/or policies; 5) representatives of organizations presenting testimony or policy.

❝We understand many possible causes of ADHD, but we do not have a definite answer regarding the actual cause.❞

—Larry B. Silver, *Attention-Deficit/Hyperactivity Disorder*. Washington, DC: American Psychiatric, 2004.

Silver is a child and adolescent psychiatrist.

❝Doctors do know that ADHD is caused by changes in brain chemicals called neurotransmitters.❞

—*TeensHealth*, "ADHD," February 2006. www.kidshealth.org.

TeensHealth is a Web site maintained by the Nemours Foundation, an organization dedicated to improving the health of children. The site offers information for youth about health, relationships, and growing up.

❝In youth with attention deficit hyperactivity disorder (ADHD), the brain matures in a normal pattern but is delayed three years in some regions, on average.❞

—National Institute of Mental Health, "Brain Matures a Few Years Late in ADHD, but Follows a Normal Pattern," press release, November 12, 2007. www.nimh.nih.gov.

The National Institute of Mental Health is the government agency dedicated to reducing the problem of mental illness and behavioral disorders, including ADHD.

❝ADHD is a highly heritable condition, as heritable as height in the human population.❞

—F. Gonzalez-Lima, "Cortical and Limbic Systems Mediating the Predisposition to Attention Deficit and Hyperactivity," quoted in Michelle P. Larimer, ed., *Attention Deficit Hyperactivity Disorder (ADHD) Research*. New York: Nova Medical, 2005.

Gonzalez-Lima is a professor at the Institute of Neurosciences, University of Texas. He specializes in neuroscience.

❝Children who have a genetic predisposition will express the disorder when put in the correct environment, typically one characterized by chaotic parenting.❞

—D. Daley, "Attention Deficit Hyperactivity Disorder: A Review of the Essential Facts," *Child: Care, Health & Development*, March 2006.

Daley is a researcher at the School of Psychology at the University of Wales in the United Kingdom.

❝Problems in parenting or parenting styles may make AD/HD better or worse, but these do not cause the disorder.❞

—National Resource Center on AD/HD, "The Disorder Named AD/HD," February 2008. www.help4adhd.org.

The National Resource Center on AD/HD is a clearinghouse for information about all aspects of ADHD.

....

❝Research suggests that prenatal exposure to tobacco, alcohol, environmental lead, and other toxins may increase the risk for ADHD.❞

—*New York Times*, "ADHD In-Depth Report," December 27, 2007. www.nytimes.com.

The *New York Times* is a daily newspaper.

....

❝There is little scientific evidence to suggest that environmental factors . . . are the underlying cause of ADD.❞

—Mental Health America, "Factsheet: AD/HD and Adults," January 9, 2007. www.mentalhealthamerica.net.

Mental Health America is an organization dedicated to helping improve the mental health of all Americans.

....

❝In the absence of objective methods for verifying the physical basis of ADHD, we . . . conceptualise ADHD as primarily a culturally constructed entity.❞

—Sami Timimi and Nick Radcliffe, "The Rise and Rise of ADHD," quoted in Craig Newnes and Nick Radcliffe, eds., *Making and Breaking Children's Lives*. Ross-On-Wye, UK: PCCS Books, 2005.

Timimi is a child and adolescent psychiatrist. Radcliffe is a clinical psychologist.

....

❝From the two studies [I conducted] it follows that the prevalence and sex ratios of ADHD in the Limpopo Province of South Africa are very similar to those reported in Western countries, which suggests that ADHD is caused by the same fundamental neurobiological processes . . . expressed independently of cultural differences.❞

—Anneke Meyer, "Cross-Cultural Issues in ADHD Research," seminar at the Centre for Advanced Studies, February 16, 2005. www.cas.uio.no.

Meyer is a professor of psychology at the University of Limpopo, South Africa.

··

❝We cannot overemphasize the point that, as a matter of science, the notion that ADHD does not exist is simply wrong.❞

—Russell A. Barkley et al., "International Consensus Statement on ADHD," *Clinical Child and Family Psychology Review,* June 2002.

Barkley is an internationally recognized authority on ADHD and has received numerous awards for his work on ADHD and in the field of psychology.

··

What Causes ADHD?

- In a June 2007 article in the *Journal of American Psychiatry* Guilherme Polanczyk et al. reveal the results of a comprehensive study of ADHD worldwide. They found that the **worldwide prevalence of ADHD is 5.2 percent.**

- The U.S. Department of Education reports that in the United States, an estimated **1.46 to 2.46 million** children (3 percent to 5 percent of the student population) have ADHD.

- According to the Mayo Clinic, research shows that children with ADHD have brains with **4 percent** smaller volume than children without ADHD.

- According to a 2007 research report by the National Institute of Mental Health, in a study of **446 children**, in some of those with ADHD certain brain regions reached greatest thickness at 10.5 years compared with only 7.5 years in children without ADHD.

- The Attention Deficit Disorder Association reports that if one person in a family has ADHD, there is a **25 to 30 percent** chance that someone else in the family will also have the disorder.

- According to the University of Maryland Medical Center, children who have ADHD usually have at least **one close relative** who also has the disorder.

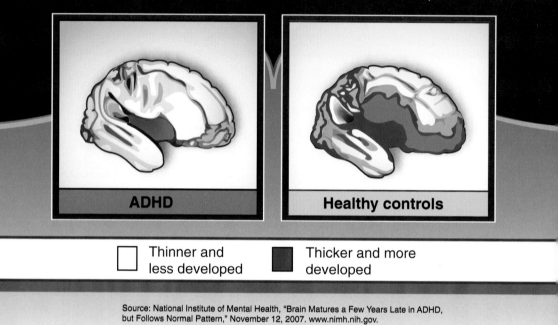

The Brain Matures More Slowly in Youth with ADHD

This comparison of an ADHD brain and a normal brain at age six shows that the middle of the brain develops later in youth with ADHD. The lighter areas are thinner and represent less developed brain tissue, while the darker areas are thicker and more developed.

ADHD

Healthy controls

☐ Thinner and less developed

■ Thicker and more developed

Source: National Institute of Mental Health, "Brain Matures a Few Years Late in ADHD, but Follows Normal Pattern," November 12, 2007. www.nimh.nih.gov.

- The University of Maryland Medical Center finds that at least **one-third** of fathers who had ADHD in their youth will have children who have ADHD.

- According to a 2006 study of 834 children by Danish researcher Karen Linnet, babies born prematurely have a **70 percent** greater risk of developing ADHD.

- A 2007 study in the *Lancet* reports that among 153 3-year-old and 144 8- and 9-year-old children, **artificial colorings and food preservatives** increased hyperactive behavior.

ADHD Is More Common in White Males

This chart, based on data from a 2006 national survey, reveals that ADHD is most common in white males. It also shows that the disorder is more common in families with highly educated parents and a high family income.

Selected characteristic	3–17 year olds with ADHD
Sex	
Male	3,352,000
Female	1,193,000
Race	
White	3,553,000
Black or African American	705,000
Asian	34,000
Native Hawaiian or other Pacific Islander	——
Hispanic or Latino	602,000
Family structure	
Mother and father	2,489,000
Mother, no father	1,611,000
Father, no mother	226,000
Neither mother nor father	219,000
Parents' education	
Less than high school diploma	406,000
High school diploma or GED	1,133,000
More than high school diploma	2,762,000
Family income	
Less than $20,000	955,000
$20,000 or more	3,409,000
$20,000–$34,999	689,000
$35,000–$54,999	646,000
$55,000–$74,999	599,000
$75,000 or more	1,045,000

Source: B. Bloom and R.A. Cohen, "Summary Health Statistics for U.S. Children: National Health Interview Survey, 2006," *National Center for Health Statistics*, 2007. www.cdc.gov.

Tobacco Smoke Is Associated with ADHD

This chart shows the results of data collected from 3,879 children, aged 4 to 15 years, and reveals that those prenatally exposed to tobacco smoke are significantly more likely to develop ADHD than those not exposed to tobacco smoke.

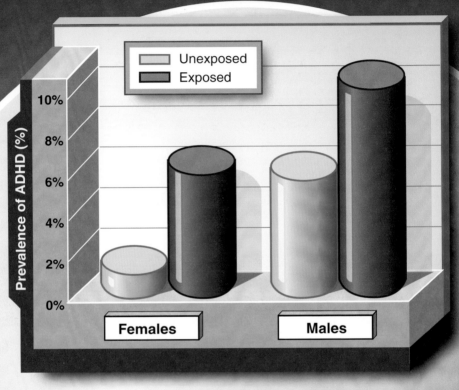

Source: Joe M. Braun et al., "Exposure to Environmental Toxicants and Attention Deficit Hyperactivity Disorder in U.S. Children," *Environmental Health Perspectives*, December 2006.

- The U.S. Centers for Disease Control and Prevention's National Center on Birth Defects and Developmental Disabilities says that ADHD is approximately **three times more common in boys** than in girls.

- In a 2006 report the National Center for Health Statistics states that of children aged 3 to 17, **9.5 percent** of boys and **5.9 percent** of girls have been diagnosed with ADHD at some time.

How Does ADHD Affect a Person's Life?

> **❝[There is a] mountain of evidence in recent years from government and academic researchers that shows AD/HD . . . can have devastating consequences if left untreated.❞**
>
> —E. Clarke Ross, "AD/HD Is Real and the Earth Is Round."

> **❝Those differences [that come with ADHD] can . . . be seen as a gift. . . . These gifts should be appreciated and developed.❞**
>
> —Lara Honos-Webb, "Interview with Dr. Honos-Webb About the Gift of ADHD."

ADHD certainly has an impact on the life of an individual and on those with whom he or she interacts. While some people argue that ADHD can be beneficial, the majority of people believe that the disorder has a negative impact on society. Whether the impact is negative or positive, ADHD does have a substantial impact on school, work, home, and social settings. It is also related to accidents and crime, depression and anxiety, and substance abuse.

School

Youth with ADHD often have difficulty in school because of the symptoms of their disorder. Inattention problems mean that children with ADHD

35

have difficulty paying attention, are easily distracted, and often fail to finish assignments on time. Hyperactivity can cause fidgeting or even running around the classroom. Finally, impulsivity often means that students with ADHD interrupt the teacher or other students and make careless errors in their schoolwork. Numerous researchers have found that youth with ADHD have lower average grades, more failing grades, more expulsions, increased dropout rates, and are less likely to graduate from high school or college. Mental Health America (MHA) points out that it is not a lack of intelligence that causes these problems in school—most children with ADHD have normal or above-normal intelligence—it is the fact that youth with ADHD have difficulty learning in a school environment. Due to the learning problems it causes, ADHD is recognized as a disability by federal legislation, and some accommodations, such as more time to take tests, may be made at school for individuals with the disorder.

Work

Research shows that ADHD frequently has a negative effect on the workplace. Brian B. Doyle, professor of psychiatry at Georgetown University in Washington, D.C., says, "Many adults with ADHD find work frustrating and disappointing. Successful work requires good executive function: organizing, planning, and following through. All of these tasks are hard for persons with ADHD."[39] Research shows that people with ADHD earn less money and lose jobs more often than those without the disorder. MHA estimates that in the United States the loss of household income for adults with ADHD is about $77 billion each year—$8,900 to $15,400 a year for the household.

> " ADHD does have a substantial impact on school, work, home, and social settings. "

However, some people point out that the enthusiasm and energy that come with ADHD can actually be an asset in the workplace. Says Blythe Grossberg, author of *Making ADD Work: On-the-Job Strategies for Coping with Attention-Deficit Disorder*, "ADD confers some significant assets—enthusiasm, extraordinary creativity, an entrepreneurial spirit, and, of course, the boundless energy for which ADDers are known. Workers who learn to capitalize on these strengths do very well, indeed."[40] She gives the example of Daniel, a man with ADHD who tried 34 different jobs before learning how to use the strengths of his ADHD to become a successful, self-employed grant writer. "Having ADD helps you make connections between things other people wouldn't see," says Daniel. "I'm constantly scanning the environment, and I always notice opportunities for business."[41]

Home

The traits associated with ADHD can strain family relationships, and people with the disorder are more likely to experience family problems. Adults with ADHD often have trouble sustaining good relationships because of their tendency to be impulsive and forgetful and to have poor communication skills. In addition, their need for stimulation may cause them to provoke conflict or to get bored with the relationship. When children struggle with ADHD, their behavior can also put stress on the family. As a *New York Times* report on ADHD explains, "The time and attention needed to deal with a child with ADHD can change internal family relationships and have devastating effects on parents and siblings. . . . It can be very difficult. A child with ADHD is wonderful one day and terrible the next, for no apparent reason."[42]

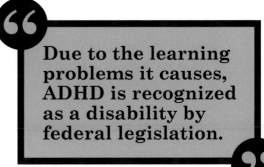

Due to the learning problems it causes, ADHD is recognized as a disability by federal legislation.

However, not all the traits associated with ADHD are negative. Marriage and family therapist Melinda White points out that people with ADHD also bring excitement and energy to others and are often creative and able to look at things with a fresh perspective. "[A person] with ADD can be quite attractive to people he meets,"[43] she says. White and others advise that family relationships do not need to fail because of ADHD; families just need to be aware of the problems the disorder may provoke and develop strategies for coping.

Social Settings

Because people with ADHD act in different ways than the majority of the population, they can have trouble in social situations. For example, people with predominantly inattentive ADHD may act shy or withdrawn. Or people with hyperactive or impulsive symptoms may act aggressively toward others. Traits such as these can make social interaction difficult. MHA explains the way ADHD can impact childhood friendships: "Other children may find it frustrating to play with a child who has ADHD, because classic symptoms include difficulty following rules, waiting one's turn or excessive talking."[44] The organization also points out that the problems people experience as a result of ADHD can cause them to be misunderstood and perceived in a negative way. It says, "Many [adults with ADHD] have been labeled as 'having a bad attitude,' 'a slow learner,' 'lacking motivation,' 'immature,' 'lazy,' 'spacey,' or 'self-centered.'"[45]

Accidents and Crime

Because they are often impulsive and/or hyperactive, people with ADHD have a higher chance of being involved in accidents. As Eric Taylor, professor at the Institute of Psychiatry at King's College London, explains, "There is plenty of evidence that people with high levels of inattentiveness, overactivity and impulsiveness are different from other people in ways that put them at risk."[46] Statistics show that people with ADHD are more likely to exhibit unsafe driving behavior. For example, according to the National Institute of Mental Health (NIMH), in their first 2 to 5 years of driving, youth with ADHD have almost 4 times as many car accidents, 3 times as many citations for speeding, and are more likely to cause bodily injury than youth without ADHD. D. Daley, researcher at the School of Psychology at the University of Wales in the United Kingdom, reviews the ADHD literature and finds that children with ADHD are more likely to be physically injured and accidentally poisoned. Research shows that as with children, adults with ADHD are also more likely to be involved in accidents.

> " The enthusiasm and energy that come with ADHD can actually be an asset in the workplace. "

A correlation between ADHD and higher rates of delinquency has also been found. The NIMH funded one of the most intensive studies on the effect of ADHD treatments, the Multimodal Treatment Study of

Children with Attention Deficit Hyperactivity Disorder (MTA). One of 4 reports issued on the study compares 487 children from the study with 272 control students and finds that in the group with ADHD, 27.1 percent showed delinquent behavior versus only 7.4 percent in the youth not diagnosed with ADHD. Former law enforcement officer Patrick Hurley and clinical psychology professor Robert Eme, authors of *Behind Bars: ADHD and Criminal Behavior*, estimate that at least one quarter of people in the criminal justice system have ADHD.

Depression and Anxiety

Both adults and children with ADHD often suffer from depression and anxiety as well. One reason is that their disorder often prevents them from functioning as they would like to or achieving their goals, and this can lead to depression and anxiety. Researchers Steven A. Safren, Carol A. Perlman, Susan Sprich, and Michael W. Otto, in their book *Mastering Your Adult ADHD* explain: "Many individuals with ADHD report a strong sense of frustration about tasks that they do not finish or do not do as well as they feel that they could have."[47] People with ADHD often have trouble with relationships, and this can also contribute to depression and anxiety. For example, researcher Kurt Robinson says, "The symptoms of ADHD often cause a child to behave in a way that annoys other children. When other children become annoyed they tend to avoid the child that creates the annoyance. Over time this can lead to a feeling of isolation for the child. . . . This isolation can lead to depression."[48]

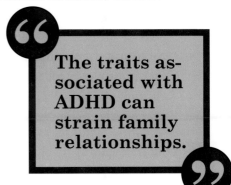

The traits associated with ADHD can strain family relationships.

Substance Abuse

Research shows that people with ADHD are more likely to develop substance-abuse problems than people without ADHD. Says Jay Giedd, chief of brain imaging at the Child Psychiatry Branch of the National Institute of Mental Health, "A plethora of epidemiologic data [indicate] that the diagnoses of ADHD and substance abuse occur together more frequently than by chance alone."[49] For example, according to ADHD expert Timothy E. Wilens, up to 25 percent of adult drug addicts and alcoholics have ADHD. A *New York Times* report on ADHD finds that approximately one in five adults with ADHD will also have substance abuse problems. Abuse can occur because people with ADHD are often impulsive and more likely to take risks, such as using illicit drugs. People with ADHD may also engage in substance abuse in an attempt to reduce their symptoms.

> " People with ADHD have a higher chance of being involved in accidents. "

Not everyone agrees that taking ADHD medication has an impact on substance abuse. Most experts believe that medication is an important way to prevent substance abuse. According to Rakesh Jain, medical doctor and assistant professor of psychiatry at the University of Houston, Texas, treatment with medication can greatly reduce the risk of future abuse. He says, "If your ADHD is well treated, your rates of misuse are significantly lower than if you have ADHD symptoms that are poorly controlled."[50] However, the effects of healthy people taking stimulants on a long-term basis has not been studied. The *New Scientist* worries, "The fear remains that today's prescribing practice may be priming millions of children for drug-dependency problems."[51] However, recent research shows that such fears may be unfounded. In 2008 the results of a 17-year study funded by the National Institutes of Health were revealed. Researchers followed a group of 176 young men who had been prescribed Ritalin for ADHD as boys. They did not find a relationship between stimulant treatment and the risk of future abuse of alcohol or other substances.

Benefits of ADHD

Some people insist that the symptoms of ADHD are not necessarily negative and that society should focus on the positive aspects of the disorder. They point out that if a person learns how to channel the extra energy that comes with ADHD, he or she can enjoy unique benefits. Says Edward M. Hallowell, psychiatrist and coauthor of *Driven to Distraction* and *Delivered from Distraction*, "ADD can become a gift—if it is unwrapped properly. People with ADD . . . usually have extraordinary talents that get buried under troubles and disappointments."[52] Researcher

Thomas Armstrong argues that people with ADHD should not be viewed as having a disability but merely as different. While people with ADHD might not have the same strengths as the majority of the population, they have different strengths, he insists. Blake Taylor is one person who has embraced the differences that come with ADHD. He spent much of his childhood trying to reduce his ADHD symptoms with medication, but he later came to believe that his condition actually gives him strengths that other people do not have. At 18 he became a best-selling author of a memoir/self-help book about living with ADHD.

However, critics insist that ADHD usually has an overall harmful impact and point out that people with ADHD are usually far more likely to experience difficulties in life than those without the disorder. According to a 2002 International Consensus Statement on ADHD made by a group of leading scientists, researchers, and clinicians who treat the disorder, "There . . . [is] incontrovertible scientific evidence that . . . [ADHD] leads to harm to the individual. Harm is established through evidence of increased mortality, morbidity, or impairment in the major life activities required of one's developmental stage in life."[53]

While exactly how ADHD impacts society is arguable, it has a significant impact on both individuals with the disorder and those they interact with. The effects of ADHD are seen in school, at work, at home, and in social settings. The disorder is also related to accidents and crime, depression and anxiety, and substance abuse.

How Does ADHD Affect a Person's Life?

❝Children with ADHD perform more poorly than their classmates. . . . These children are more likely to fail subjects, to be held back, and to drop out of school.❞

—Richard Milich, Elizabeth P. Lorch, and Kristen S. Berthiaume, "Story Comprehension in Children with ADHD: Research Findings and Treatment Implications," quoted in Michelle P. Larimer, ed., *Attention Deficit Hyperactivity Disorder (ADHD) Research.* New York: Nova Medical, 2005.

Milich, Lorch, and Berthiaume are researchers at the University of Kentucky,

---

❝The everyday tasks of getting up, getting dressed and ready for the day's work, getting to work on time, and being productive on the job can be major challenges for the ADD adult.❞

—National Institute of Mental Health, "Attention Deficit Hyperactivity Disorder," 2006. www.nimh.nih.gov.

The National Institute of Mental Health is the government agency dedicated to reducing the problem of mental illness and behavioral disorders, including ADHD.

---

* Editor's Note: While the definition of a primary source can be narrowly or broadly defined, for the purposes of Compact Research, a primary source consists of: 1) results of original research presented by an organization or researcher; 2) eyewitness accounts of events, personal experience, or work experience; 3) first-person editorials offering pundits' opinions; 4) government officials presenting political plans and/or policies; 5) representatives of organizations presenting testimony or policy.

❝In some fields . . . the unique wiring of the ADD brain is a competitive advantage.❞

—Pete Quily, "Top 10 Advantages of ADD in a High Tech Career," *Adult ADD Strengths*, February 9, 2006. http://adultaddstrengths.com.

Quily has ADHD. He also coaches adults with the disorder and maintains a Web site with ADHD resources.

❝The time and attention needed to deal with a child with ADHD can change internal family relationships and have devastating effects on parents and siblings.❞

—*New York Times*, "ADHD In-Depth Report," December 27, 2007. www.nytimes.com.

The *New York Times* is a daily newspaper.

❝Many adults with ADHD report a life full of problems and frustrations. . . . Others often perceive behaviors related to ADHD as the result of being *lazy*, *stupid*, or just *difficult*.❞

—Philip J. Asheron and J.J. Sandra Kooij, "The Clinical Assessment and Treatment of ADHD in Adults," quoted in Eric Taylor, ed., *People with Hyperactivity: Understanding and Managing Their Problems*. London: Mac Keith, 2007.

Asheron is professor of molecular psychiatry at King's College London and Kooij is a consultant psychiatrist and head of the Department of Psychiatry at Den Haag in the Netherlands.

❝[A person] with ADD can be quite attractive to people he meets. He brings excitement and energy to life. He knows how to have fun and may show a wonderful sense of humor.❞

—Melinda White, "How Adult ADHD Affects Relationships: Strategies for Coping," *ADD Consults*, October 20, 2004. www.addconsults.com.

White is a marriage and family therapist.

❝A meta-analysis . . . evaluating the relationship between ADHD status and various driving behaviors and outcomes was performed. . . . Results from these . . . studies generally indicate there is an association between individuals with ADHD and increased driving risk.❞

—Lawrence Jerome, Alvin Segal, and Liat Habinski, "What We Know About ADHD and Driving Risk: A Literature Review, Meta-Analysis and Critique," *Journal of the Canadian Academy of Child and Adolescent Psychiatry*, August 2006.

Jerome is a researcher in the Department of Psychiatry, Segal is from the Department of Psychology, and Habinski is from the Department of Epidemiology and Biostatistics at the University of Western Ontario in Canada.

❝In juvenile offenders, estimates of incidence of ADHD reach 30% . . . as compared to the 3–5% expected in the general population.❞

—Janet R. Schultz, "Behavioral Treatment for Youth with Conduct Disorder," quoted in W.M. Nelson III, A.J. Finch Jr., and K.J. Hart, *Conduct Disorders: A Practitioner's Guide to Comparative Treatments*. New York: Springer, 2006.

Schultz is a psychologist who specializes in behavioral medicine, pediatric psychology, and psychotherapy with children.

❝Attention deficit hyperactivity disorder may make a child depressed . . . because parents and teachers and peers are always giving them a hard time for how they're acting.❞

—Nadine Kaslow, "Section 3: Diagnosis: How Is Depression Diagnosed in Children?" *ABC News OnCall+ Mind and Mood: Depression Center!* February 27, 2008. www.abcnews.go.com.

Kaslow is a professor of psychiatry at the Emory University School of Medicine in Georgia.

❝As an ADHD adult . . . I suffer from periodic depression and anxiety.❞

—Michele Haynes, "ADHD, Depression, Anxiety: Is It a Heart Problem?" *ADHD of the Christian Kind*, 2007. www.christianadhd.com.

Haynes is an adult with ADHD.

66 Here we have a condition which, if you treat it [with medication] . . . your risk of turning to substance abuse . . . [is] cut in half. 99

—Rakesh Jain, interviewed by Richard Weisler, "ADHD and Substance Use Disorders: An Expert Interview with Richard Weisler, MD, and Rakesh Jain, MD, MPH," *Medscape*, November 29, 2006. www.medscape.com.

Jain is a medical doctor and assistant professor of psychiatry at the University of Houston, Texas.

66 The fear remains that today's prescribing practice [to treat ADHD] may be priming millions of children for drug-dependency problems. 99

—*New Scientist*, "Attention Please: The Way We Deal with Hyperactivity Disorder Leaves a Lot to Be Desired," April 1, 2006.

New Scientist is a print and online magazine that provides science and technology news from around the world.

66 As the father of a 17-year-old son with AD/HD . . . I know the disorder can make every day a struggle for happiness and success. 99

—E. Clarke Ross, "AD/HD Is Real and the Earth Is Round," *CHADD Leadership Blog*, November 19, 2007. http://chaddleadershipblog.blogspot.com.

Ross is chief executive officer of the organization Children and Adults with Attention-Deficit/Hyperactivity Disorder.

66 Children with ADHD have capacities that other children do not have. These gifts should be appreciated and developed. 99

—Lara Honos-Webb, "Interview with Dr. Honos-Webb About the Gift of ADHD," *Visionary Soul*. www.visionarysoul.com.

Honos-Webb is a clinical psychologist in California. She is author of *The Gift of ADHD* and more than 25 scholarly articles.

How Does ADHD Affect a Person's Life?

- In a 2005 survey of 1,000 American adults, conducted by Roper Public Affairs, researchers found that **17 percent** of the adults with ADHD did not graduate from high school, compared with **7 percent** of those without ADHD.

- ADHD expert Russell A. Barkley reports that **21 percent** of teens with ADHD skip school on a regular basis.

- Mental Health America estimates that in the United States the loss of household income for adults with ADHD is about **$77 billion** each year.

- In a 2008 report in *Occupational and Environmental Medicine*, researchers report the results of interviews with 7,075 workers aged 18 to 44 in 10 countries. They state that in the United States ADHD costs an average of **28.3 days** performance each year.

- According to Mental Health America, adults with ADHD are twice as likely to be **separated or divorced**.

- According to the National Institute of Mental Health, in the first 2 to 5 years of driving, youth with ADHD have **3 times as many citations for speeding** as those without ADHD.

ADHD Affects a Person in Many Ways

The American Psychiatric Association provides the criteria for diagnosing ADHD, of which an abbreviated list is included here. These symptoms must be present for at least six months and be disruptive and inappropriate for developmental level. As this list shows, ADHD can be harmful in many facets of a person's life.

Inattention

1.) Often does not give close attention to details or makes careless mistakes in schoolwork, work, or other activities.

2.) Often has trouble keeping attention on tasks or play activities.

3.) Often does not seem to listen when spoken to directly.

4.) Often does not follow instructions and fails to finish schoolwork, chores, or duties in the workplace (not due to oppositional behavior or failure to understand instructions).

5.) Often has trouble organizing information.

6.) Often avoids, dislikes, or doesn't want to do things that take a lot of mental effort for a long period of time (e.g., schoolwork and homework).

7.) Often loses things needed for tasks and activities (e.g., toys, school assignments, pencils, books, and tools).

8.) Is often easily distracted.

9.) Is often forgetful in daily activities.

Hyperactivity

1.) Often fidgets with hands or feet or squirms in seat.

2.) Often gets up from seat when remaining in seat is expected.

3.) Often runs about or climbs when and where it is not appropriate (adolescents or adults may feel restless).

4.) Often has trouble playing or enjoying leisure activities quietly.

5.) Is often "on the go" or often acts as if "driven by a motor."

6.) Often talks excessively.

Impulsivity

4.) Often blurts out answers before questions have been finished.

5.) Often has trouble waiting one's turn.

6.) Often interrupts or intrudes on others (e.g., butts into conversations or games).

Source: Centers for Disease Control and Prevention, "Attention-Deficit/ Hyperactivity Disorder–Symptoms of ADHD," no date. www.cdc.gov.

ADHD Has a Significant Impact on Children Around the World

This maps shows select results of worldwide ADHD prevalence studies conducted between 1992 and 2005. It reveals that reported rates of ADHD among school-aged children are significant, and range between 4 and 14 percent.

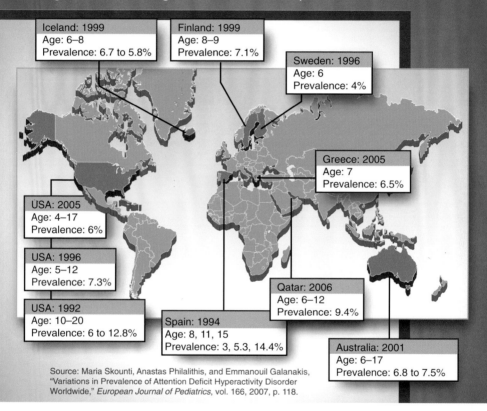

Iceland: 1999
Age: 6–8
Prevalence: 6.7 to 5.8%

Finland: 1999
Age: 8–9
Prevalence: 7.1%

Sweden: 1996
Age: 6
Prevalence: 4%

Greece: 2005
Age: 7
Prevalence: 6.5%

USA: 2005
Age: 4–17
Prevalence: 6%

USA: 1996
Age: 5–12
Prevalence: 7.3%

USA: 1992
Age: 10–20
Prevalence: 6 to 12.8%

Spain: 1994
Age: 8, 11, 15
Prevalence: 3, 5.3, 14.4%

Qatar: 2006
Age: 6–12
Prevalence: 9.4%

Australia: 2001
Age: 6–17
Prevalence: 6.8 to 7.5%

Source: Maria Skounti, Anastas Philalithis, and Emmanouil Galanakis, "Variations in Prevalence of Attention Deficit Hyperactivity Disorder Worldwide," *European Journal of Pediatrics*, vol. 166, 2007, p. 118.

- Mental Health America reports that adults with ADHD are **four times more likely to be involved in an automobile accident.**

- In a 2006 survey of 526 parents of children with ADHD, the United Kingdom's National Attention Deficit Disorder Information and Support Service found that **19 percent** of children with ADHD have been in trouble with the police.

- A 2004 survey of 1,001 adults by Roper ASW found that **40 percent** of adults with ADHD strongly agree that they have a bright future, and **50 percent** like being themselves, compared to **67 percent** and **76 percent** of adults without the disorder.

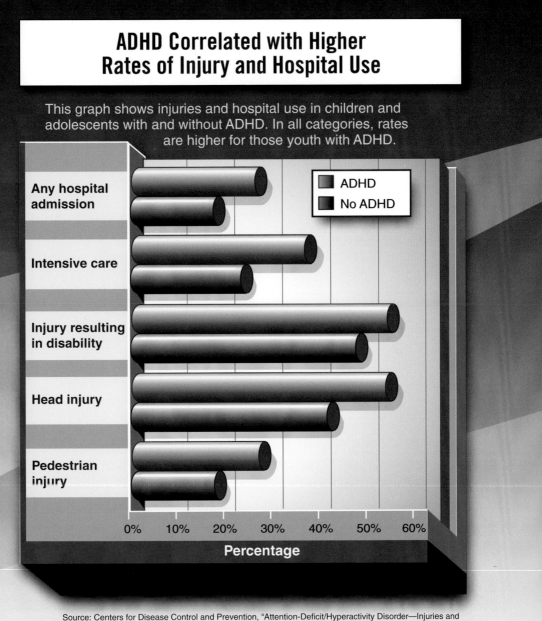

ADHD Correlated with Higher Rates of Injury and Hospital Use

This graph shows injuries and hospital use in children and adolescents with and without ADHD. In all categories, rates are higher for those youth with ADHD.

Legend:
- ADHD
- No ADHD

Categories (y-axis):
- Any hospital admission
- Intensive care
- Injury resulting in disability
- Head injury
- Pedestrian injury

Percentage (x-axis): 0% 10% 20% 30% 40% 50% 60%

Source: Centers for Disease Control and Prevention, "Attention-Deficit/Hyperactivity Disorder—Injuries and ADHD," no date. www.cdc.gov.

ADHD Is Associated with Many Impairments

This chart shows some of the most common ways that ADHD can have a harmful impact on individuals at different stages of life.

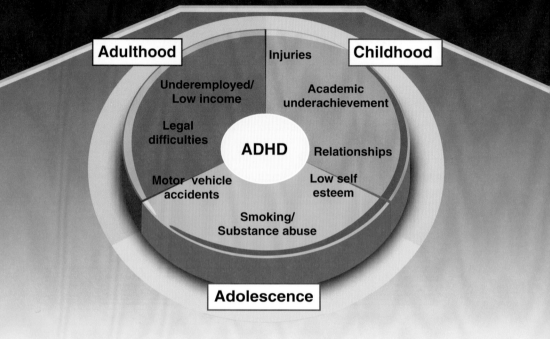

Source: Teach ADHD, "Myths and Facts about ADHD," no date. http://research.aboutkidshealth.ca.

- A 2004 survey of 1,001 adults by Roper ASW, supported by Shire US Inc., found that **52 percent** of those with ADHD are currently employed, versus **72 percent** of those without the disorder.

- In 2008 Joseph Biederman et al. reported the results of a study of 112 young men with ADHD who were assessed 10 years after their initial diagnosis. The researchers found that the use of **stimulant drugs** has no effect on the risk of future substance abuse.

- According to ADHD expert Timothy E. Wilens, adults with ADHD are twice as likely to have **substance abuse disorders** compared to those without ADHD.

How Should ADHD Be Treated?

> **"Although medication can be effective in treating ADHD symptoms, many parents of ADHD children and adults with ADHD want treatments that can supplement medication or reduce its necessity."**
>
> —UCLA Neuropsychiatric Institute, Program on ADHD and Related Conditions, "Meditation-Based Intervention for Attention Deficit Hyperactivity Disorder: The UCLA Mindful Awareness Program (MAP)."

> **"Most children with ADHD benefit from taking medication. . . . Medications for ADHD are well established and effective."**
>
> —American Academy of Child and Adolescent Psychiatry, "ADHD—a Guide for Families."

One of the most intensive studies of ADHD treatments in the United States is the Multimodal Treatment Study of Children with Attention Deficit Hyperactivity Disorder, funded by the National Institute of Mental Health (NIMH). In this study, researchers followed 579 elementary school children and found that three years after starting treatment for ADHD, children continue to experience improvement in their symptoms whether they use medication only, behavioral therapy, or a combination. This indicates that the most effective way to improve ADHD symptoms is to undergo some type of treatment. However, exactly which treatment is most effective is still in dispute. Widespread debate continues over the effectiveness and safety of stimulants and other medication and over alternatives to medication, such as education and therapy, exercise and diet, and biofeedback.

Stimulants

Extensively debated is whether medication—the most common treatment for ADHD—is the best treatment for the disorder. Many people insist that stimulants have been proved safe and effective. Mental Health America says that 9 out of 10 children respond positively to ADHD medication, and 50 percent of those who do not respond to the first medication will respond to a second option. The organization calls long-acting, once-daily stimulant medications the "gold standard" of medical therapy. According to William Barbaresi, a developmental and behavioral pediatrician at the Mayo Clinic, more research is available on ADHD medicines than on many other medicines commonly prescribed in the United States. He says, "ADHD medications have been prescribed longer than most every other class of medications currently available."[54]

> **Exactly which [ADHD] treatment is most effective is still in dispute.**

However, many criticize stimulants. Concerns about prescribing these drugs to children and adults include potential side effects such as decreased appetite, insomnia, nervousness, headache, rapid heart rate, and mood swings. In addition, this class of medication does not improve ADHD symptoms in some people. The NIMH says that approximately 1 in 10 children is not helped by stimulant medication. Some people also question whether it is appropriate to give powerful stimulant drugs to people on a regular basis. Psychologist Lawrence Weathers, author of *ADHD: A Path to Success*, says,

> It is important to realize that all of the stimulant drugs prescribed for ADHD/ADD are closely related to some illegal street drugs. These include dextroamphetamine (dexedrine) (street name: 'dexies'), methamphetamine (street name: 'crystal meth'), and, of course, cocaine. We imprison people for making drugs very similar to the drugs we prescribe to our ADHD children.[55]

Lawyer Gerald K. McOscar suggests that with all the potential side effects, stimulant treatment might be worse than living with ADHD. He says, "Wouldn't (shouldn't) it be child abuse per se to prescribe mind altering drugs with potentially serious or fatal psychiatric effects to . . . children, no matter how challenged . . . or challenging?"[56]

Stimulants and Heart Problems

One potentially serious side effect of stimulant medication is the possibility that it may increase the risk of cardiac problems, including sudden death from heart failure. In 2006 a U.S. Food and Drug Administration (FDA) advisory committee reviewed the evidence on stimulants and heart risks. It found that between 1999 and 2003, 25 people taking ADHD medications died suddenly, and 43 experienced cardiovascular problems including strokes, cardiac arrest, and heart palpitations. The committee recommended that the drugs include a "black box" warning about possible cardiovascular risks. However, later that year the FDA Pediatric Advisory Committee reviewed the evidence and did not follow the recommendation for a black box warning. The issue of stimulants and heart problems came back into public debate in 2008, when the American Heart Association made a statement advising that before taking stimulants to treat ADHD, children should have a heart workup, including an electrocardiogram, to detect any potential heart problems.

However, many doctors insist that taking stimulants presents no significant risk for heart problems. In the December 2007 volume of *Pediatrics* Almut G. Winterstein et al. analyzed information from Florida Medicaid files and used data on more than 55,000 children aged 3 to 20 diagnosed with ADHD. The researchers found that children taking stimulants are more likely to visit the doctor or emergency department for cardiac problems, but that stimulants do not appear to be a significant cause of hospital admission or death. They conclude: "The incidence of fatal and serious events because of circulatory causes in the study population was low and seemed similar to national background rates."[57] In response to warnings about cardiac problems associated with ADHD medications, psychiatrist Edward M. Hallowell argues that, like any medication, stimulants can be dangerous when used improperly, "But keep perspective," he says, "Aspirin is more danger-

> " Many people insist that stimulants have been proved safe and effective. "

ous for adults than stimulants. And penicillin is estimated to kill 500 to 1,000 people each year. Yet we rightly revere aspirin and penicillin, while cautioning that they be used with care. No black box needed.[58]

Strattera

Nonstimulant medication Strattera (atomoxetine) became available in 2003 in the United States to treat ADHD in children over 6 and in adults. However, in 2005 the FDA warned of an increased risk of suicidal thinking in youth being treated with Strattera, and the drug now carries a warning label on the medication stating, "In some children and teens, Strattera increases the risk of suicidal thoughts." According to Eli Lilly and Company, the manufacturer of the drug, in clinical trials suicidal thoughts were observed only in about 4 out of every 1,000 patients, and no suicides occurred. The company states that it found no indication of an increased suicide risk in adults. Strattera can also cause severe liver problems in rare cases. Despite the rarity of reported side effects, some people are very critical of the safety of Strattera. For example, the Web site *Death from Ritalin*, which is opposed to the use of medication to treat ADHD, offers numerous testimonials on its adverse effects. One parent says, "After approximately 7 weeks [of taking Strattera, my son] . . . began being plagued by thoughts of death: fear of dying . . . worried about the world exploding and everyone dying. . . . He cried that he wished he could just go back to how he used to be before these thoughts started." Another parent says, "Two of my three children were given Strattera upon the medication's release. Both of them had violent outbursts (unheard of from either of them), severe nausea, headaches, and horrible mood swings. Upon discontinuation of this medication, all of these symptoms were gone."[59]

> "Stimulant medication . . . may increase the risk of cardiac problems."

Other Medications

When stimulant medications are not effective, doctors sometimes prescribe other drugs that are not FDA approved to treat ADHD but have proven effective at reducing its symptoms in certain people. These other drugs are not generally as effective as stimulants; however, doctors often consider them to be a good option for people who do not benefit from stimulants. This type of treatment is called off-label use. Several antidepressants are used to treat ADHD symptoms. These drugs work by increasing levels of certain neurotransmitters, similar to stimulants, and so they can have a similar effect on ADHD as stimulants. Some drugs used to treat high blood pressure—antihypertensives—have also been found effective in ADHD treatment. In addition, numerous antipsychotic medications are used. Like stimulants, these other types of medication also have side effects which vary by drug but can include headaches, nausea, and insomnia.

> **Several antidepressants are used to treat ADHD symptoms.**

In a report on ADHD medication, *Consumer Reports* points out that many of these alternative drugs have a significantly higher risk of adverse side effects than stimulants and warns, "We recommend that the medicines not approved to treat ADHD be used *very cautiously*."[60]

Effects of Medication on Mood

How ADHD medications affect the mood and personality of the person taking them is also controversial. Many medical professionals insist that these medications should have no adverse effects. For example, Larry B. Silver, child and adolescent psychiatrist, says that the drugs simply allow the brain to function normally. He states, "Parents need to understand that the medications used do not drug, sedate, or tranquilize the individual. These medications correct an underlying neurochemical deficiency and allow the individual to function normally."[61]

However, statements such as this are contradicted by the stories of people who have actually taken these medications. In an October 2006 study in the *Journal for Specialists in Pediatric Nursing*, Julie B. Meaux et al. interviewed 15 college students about their experiences with ADHD medication. The researchers found the participants describing a "trade-off" experience with stimulant medication—the medication helped them in school, but it made them feel worse in other ways. Say the authors, "They described that even as children they didn't like the way the medications made them feel. 'I would get work done, but I was just so far out of it.'"[62] Some participants believe that medication actually hurt them in school because it took away their creativity.

Medication for Adults

As ADHD becomes more widely discussed in society, an increasing number of adults are becoming aware that they may have the disorder and wondering about medication to treat it. However, more evidence on the effectiveness and safety of stimulants for adults is needed. According to researchers Steven A. Safren, Carol A. Perlman, Susan Sprich, and Michael W. Otto, medication is less effective in adults than children. They say,

> Although medications are highly useful in the treatment of adult ADHD, it appears that they are only partially effective. In . . . studies . . . 20–50 percent of adults are considered nonresponders due to insufficient symptom reduction or inability to tolerate these medications. . . . Moreover, adults who are considered responders typically show a reduction in only 50 percent or fewer of the core symptoms of ADHD, and these response rates are worse than the rates found in children. . . . This means that many residual symptoms often persist for adults with ADHD after adequate medication treatment.[63]

In addition, other researchers point out that while youth using medication may grow out of the disorder and stop taking that medication, adults will most likely have the disorder for the rest of their lives and thus be taking medication for the rest of their lives. Medical experts are unsure about the impact of using ADHD drugs for so long. However, many people believe that while medication might have some potential problems, it is still the best option.

In comparison to the fact that an increasing number of adults are using stimulants, many youth actually stop taking them as they become adults. While ADHD symptoms often continue into adulthood, many youth stop taking medication to treat their symptoms because they prefer the way they feel without it, and they believe they can learn to manage their symptoms better. According to research conducted by Mariellen Fischer, professor of neurology at the Medical College of Wisconsin, 9 in

10 ADHD sufferers are off their medication by the time they reach 21. For example, Devin Barclay began taking Ritalin at age 7. At 23 years old, off Ritalin for 7 years, he says, "I felt like a happier person. I just felt more like myself."[64]

Education and Therapy

Most people agree that education and therapy can be helpful to people with ADHD and to those who interact with them. One element of education and therapy involves teaching the person with ADHD how to better understand his or her behavior and showing him or her skills to cope with the symptoms of the disorder. These skills include maintaining a consistent schedule, learning how to minimize distractions, and using tools to stay organized. Many people point out that it is also important to teach a person with ADHD to utilize his or her strengths. Says Hallowell, "The most powerful help is the identification and development of their strengths. I have seen this, more than any other intervention, transform patients' lives."[65]

> " How ADHD medications affect the mood and personality of the person taking them is . . . controversial. "

In addition to teaching the person with ADHD, family, teachers, and friends can be taught to understand what it is like to have ADHD and how to deal with people who have the disorder. The National Alliance on Mental Illness emphasizes that in order to successfully treat a person with ADHD, "It is extremely important for family members and teachers or employers to remain patient and understanding."[66]

Other Approaches

Numerous other ADHD treatments exist in addition to medication, education, and therapy. These include special diets; for example, adding certain nutritional supplements or eliminating foods such as sugar, artificial colors, flavors, preservatives, and common allergens such as wheat or milk. Some people say that regular exercise helps control the symptoms of ADHD. Others believe chiropractic adjustments can help with the disorder. Some people also recommend limiting television and video games. Biofeedback, or neurofeedback, a stress-reduction technique that teaches people to learn to control certain body responses, has been used to teach those with ADHD to change their brain wave patterns to ones that are more normal.

However, support for the alternative treatments is often anecdotal rather than scientirfic, and so many people favor medication over these unproven alternatives. For example, in the opinion of psychiatrist Randy Ross, "Medication consistently turns out to be very helpful and very effective . . . with minimal side effects." He argues that "other forms of treatment are not as well studied and in general tend to be minimally effective."[67]

While medication has become an increasingly common treatment for ADHD, researchers, medical professionals, and people with ADHD continue to disagree over the effectiveness and safety of stimulants and other types of medication, and over alternatives such as education and therapy, exercise and diet, and biofeedback.

How Should ADHD Be Treated?

"The best long-term research clearly indicates that stimulant treatment is the most effective currently available treatment for individuals who have ADHD."

> —Mayo Clinic, interview with William Barbaresi, "ADHD Medications: Are They Safe?" April 20, 2006.
> www.mayoclinic.com.

Barbaresi is a developmental and behavioral pediatrician at the Mayo Clinic in Rochester, Minnesota.

....

"Taking drugs is not always the route to success. Short-term studies find that children do concentrate better if they take drugs to calm them. Yet there is no convincing evidence that they have better grades as they leave secondary school than ADHD children who do not take drugs."

> —*Economist*, "Desperate Parents, Dangerous Drugs; Hyperactive Children," April 22, 2006.

The *Economist* is an online and print newsmagazine offering analysis and commentary of world business and current affairs.

....

* Editor's Note: While the definition of a primary source can be narrowly or broadly defined, for the purposes of Compact Research, a primary source consists of: 1) results of original research presented by an organization or researcher; 2) eyewitness accounts of events, personal experience, or work experience; 3) first-person editorials offering pundits' opinions; 4) government officials presenting political plans and/or policies; 5) representatives of organizations presenting testimony or policy.

❝ Optimal treatment for ADHD is still a matter of debate. ❞

—Mayo Clinic, "Attention-Deficit/Hyperactivity Disorder (ADHD)," February 16, 2007. www.mayoclinic.com.

The Mayo Clinic is a nonprofit medical practice that also works to provide reliable health information on a variety of topics, including ADHD.

❝ The FDA has an ethical duty to warn the millions of adults and children currently taking ADHD drugs, or who might be prescribed the drugs in the future, that the drugs may be deadly. ❞

—*HealthFacts*, "From the Director . . . : Warning Label Advised for Hyperactivity Drugs," April 2006.

HealthFacts is a monthly newsletter published by the Center for Medical Consumers that offers a critical perspective on recent medical news.

❝ This study [found that] . . . the incidence of fatal and serious events because of circulatory causes in the study population was low [among those people using stimulants] and seemed similar to national background rates. ❞

—Almut G. Winterstein et al., "Cardiac Safety of Central Nervous System Stimulants in Children and Adolescents with Attention-Deficit/Hyperactivity Disorder," *Pediatrics*, December 2007. http://pediatrics.aappublications.org.

Winterstein et al. are researchers from the University of Florida in Gainesville. Zito is from the University of Maryland in Baltimore.

❝ After a diagnosis of ADHD has been made but before therapy with a stimulant or other medication is initiated, a thorough evaluation [of any cardiac conditions] should be performed. ❞

—Victoria L. Vetter et al., "Cardiovascular Monitoring of Children and Adolescents with Heart Disease Receiving Stimulant Drugs: A Scientific Statement from the American Heart Association Council on Cardiovascular Disease in the Young Congenital Cardiac Defects Committee and the Council on Cardiovascular Nursing," *Circulation*, April 21, 2008.

The authors are affiliated with the American Heart Association, an organization that works to reduce cardiovascular heart disease and strokes in the United States.

❝Strattera provides uninterrupted relief from ADHD symptoms throughout the day into the evening. . . . [In studies of the effects of the drug] Strattera was generally well-tolerated.❞

—Eli Lilly and Company, "First Medication Indicated for Maintenance Treatment for ADHD," May 8, 2008. www.strattera.com.

Eli Lilly and Company is a pharmaceutical company that manufactures numerous pharmaceuticals, including the ADHD medication Strattera.

....

❝We recommend that the medicines not approved to treat ADHD be used *very cautiously*.❞

—Consumers Union, "Consumer Reports Best Buy Drugs: Evaluating Prescription Drugs Used to Treat Attention Deficit Hyperactivity Disorder; Comparing Effectiveness, Safety, and Price," 2005.

The Consumers Union is an organization whose goal is to provide consumers with unbiased information on various goods and services.

....

❝Both male and female participants used similar words to describe the medications as making them feel 'somber' or 'mellow.' . . . [A] female participant described feeling 'that everything is just OK all the time. It's never great and it's never terrible. It's like I'm monotone the whole day long.'❞

—Julie B. Meaux, Carla Hester, Billy Smith, and Amy Shoptaw, "Stimulant Medications: A Trade-Off? The Lived Experiences of Adolescents with ADHD," *Journal for Specialists in Pediatric Nursing*, October 2006.

Meaux is associate professor of nursing at the University of Central Arkansas, Hester is a clinical nurse specialist at the University of Arkansas for Medical Sciences, Smith is a professor of psychology, and Shoptaw is a research assistant at the University of Central Arkansas.

....

❝[A] common misconception is that stimulants turn children into 'zombies.' Proper doses of medication increase concentration, decrease hyperactivity and seem to exert a calming effect, sleepiness or unresponsiveness is not typical unless the child is greatly over-medicated.❞

—Ernest J. Bordini, "Attention-Deficit Hyperactivity Disorder (ADHD) Medication: A Growing List of Choices," Clinical Psychology Associates of North Central Florida, March 30, 2005. http://cpancf.com.

Bordini is executive director of Clinical Psychology Associates of North Central Florida and a neuropsychologist who specializes in assessment of ADHD as well as head injuries.

❝Although medications are highly useful in the treatment of adult ADHD, it appears that they are only partially effective. In . . . studies . . . 20–50 percent of adults are considered nonresponders due to insufficient symptom reduction or inability to tolerate these medications.❞

—Steven A. Safren, Carol A. Perlman, Susan Sprich, and Michael W. Otto, *Mastering Your Adult ADHD: A Cognitive-Behavioral Treatment Program.* New York: Oxford University Press, 2005.

Safren is director of Behavioral Medicine Service, Perlman and Sprich are clinical assistants in psychology, and Otto is director of the Cognitive-Behavioral Therapy Program, at Massachusetts General Hospital.

❝Medication is no panacea. . . . Other treatments are often necessary—some would say always necessary—to effectively treat ADHD. An important non-medical approach used in treating children with ADHD is known as behavior therapy or behavior management.❞

—David Rabiner, "Behavioral Treatment for ADHD: An Overview," *At Health*, February 1, 2007. www.athealth.com.

Rabiner is a clinical child psychologist who specializes in the evaluation and treatment of children with ADHD. He teaches and conducts research at Duke University in North Carolina.

"The most effective treatments for ADHD include a combination of medication, behavioral therapy, and parental support and education."

—Mental Health America, "Factsheet: AD/HD and Kids," July 18, 2007. www.mentalhealthamerica.com.

Mental Health America is an organization dedicated to helping improve the mental health of all Americans.

"Food dyes and other ingredients contribute to behavioral disorders in a large ... number of children. Eliminating those ingredients could mitigate the need for many children to take Ritalin or other stimulant drugs."

—Michael F. Jacobson, testimony at Public Hearing on Food Additives and Behavioral Disorders, Assembly Standing Committee on Mental Health, Mental Retardation, and Developmental Disabilities, New York State Assembly, New York, October 30, 2007.

Jacobson is executive director of the Center for Science in the Public Interest, an organization that works to counter the influence of private industry on public opinion.

"Those treatments not scientifically proven to work [for treatment of ADHD] include ... special diets, allergy treatment, [and] megavitamins."

—National Alliance on Mental Illness, "Attention-Deficit/Hyperactivity Disorder," 2008. www.nami.org.

The National Alliance on Mental Illness is an organization dedicated to eradicating mental illness.

How Should ADHD Be Treated?

- According to the Centers for Disease Control and Prevention, in 2003 an estimated **2.5 million** children in the United States took medication for ADHD.

- The National Alliance on Mental Illness reports that medication is effective for the short term treatment of more than **76 percent** of people with ADHD.

- The National Institute of Mental Health reports that approximately **10 percent** of children are not helped by stimulant medication.

- According to *Consumer Reports*, **60 to 80 percent** of youth who take stimulants become less hyperactive and impulsive, better able to focus, and less disruptive at home or school.

- The November 2006 issue of the *Journal of the American Academy of Child and Adolescent Psychiatry* reports that in a study of 303 preschoolers taking stimulants for ADHD, **10 percent** of children had to drop out of the study due to intolerable side effects, including weight loss, insomnia, and mood disturbances.

- In 2008 the *Wall Street Journal* reported that since 1999, fewer than 30 children have had a **sudden cardiac arrest** linked to stimulants.

ADHD Is Commonly Treated with Stimulant Medication

This list shows the stimulants commonly used to treat ADHD, with their trade—or brand—names, their generic names, and the age for which they are approved for treatment by the U.S. Food and Drug Administration.

Trade Name	Generic Name	Approved Age
Adderall	amphetamine	3 and older
Concerta	methylphenidate (long acting)	6 and older
Cylert	pemoline	6 and older
Dexedrine	dextroamphetamine	3 and older
Dextrostat	dextroamphetamine	3 and older
Focalin	dexmethylphendiate	6 and older
Metadate ER	methylphenidate (extended release)	6 and older
Metadate CD	methylphenidate (extended release)	6 and older
Ritalin	methylphenidate	6 and older
Ritalin SR	methylphenidate (extended release)	6 and older
Ritalin LA	methylphenidate (long acting)	6 and older

Source: National Institute of Mental Health, "Attention Deficit Hyperactivity Disorder," 2006. www.nimh.nih.gov.

- In a 2007 study in *Pediatrics*, researchers Almut G. Winterstein et al. report that stimulant use is associated with a **20 percent** increase in the likelihood of emergency department visits for a cardiac problem.

- According to Eli Lilly and Company, in clinical trials of Strattera suicidal thoughts were observed in **4 out of every 1,000** children and teens taking the medication.

ADHD Stimulant Prescriptions in the United States Have Increased

This graph shows the total number of stimulant prescriptions dispensed by U.S. pharmacies between 1991 and 2007. Stimulants are primarily prescribed for the treatment of ADHD. According to this data, the total has increased sevenfold, from approximately 5 million in 1991, to almost 35 million in 2007.

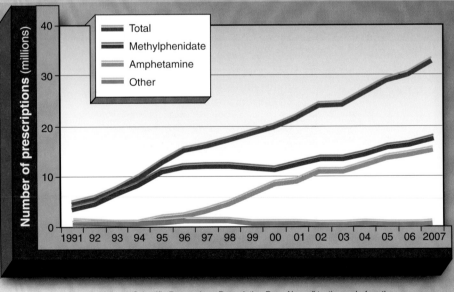

Source: Nora D. Volkow, "Scientific Research on Prescription Drug Abuse," testimony before the Subcommittee on Crime and Drugs, Committee on the Judiciary and the Caucus on International Narcotics Control, United States Senate, March 12, 2008. www.nida.nih.gov.

ADHD Stimulants Are Associated with Emergency Department Visits

According to this graph, there are a significant number of emergency department (ED) visits due to both medical and nonmedical (without a prescription) use of ADHD stimulant medications.

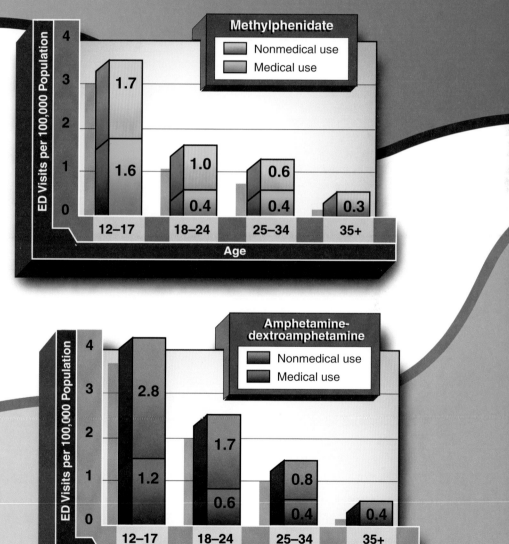

Methylphenidate
- Nonmedical use
- Medical use

ED Visits per 100,000 Population / Age

Age	Nonmedical use	Medical use
12–17	1.6	1.7
18–24	0.4	1.0
25–34	0.4	0.6
35+		0.3

Amphetamine-dextroamphetamine
- Nonmedical use
- Medical use

ED Visits per 100,000 Population / Age

Age	Nonmedical use	Medical use
12–17	1.2	2.8
18–24	0.6	1.7
25–34	0.4	0.8
35+		0.4

Source: Substance Abuse and Mental Health Services Administration, "Emergency Department Visits Involving ADHD Stimulant Medications," *The New DAWN Report,* issue 29, 2006. http://dawninfo.samhsa.gov.

ADHD Stimulants Are Not a Major Risk Factor for Cardiac Problems

This chart reveals the results of a study that investigated the link between ADHD and cardiac problems. In data from Florida Medicaid claims between 1994 and 2004, of youth 3 to 20 years old diagnosed with ADHD, 55,383 were included in the study, with a total of 124,932 person-years of observation. Researchers found that emergency department and physician visits are similar for people with ADHD who are taking stimulants and those who are not using stimulants.

Emergency Department Visit	Person-years	Cardiac event
Current use	42,612	406
Former use	36,671	261
Non use	46,649	424
Physician Office Visit		
Current use	42,637	440
Former use	35,479	291
Non use	46,399	503

Source: Almut G. Winterstein et al., "Cardiac Safety of Central Nervous System Stimulants in Children and Adolescents with Attention-Deficit/Hyperactivity Disorder," *Pediatrics*, December 2007. http://pediatrics.aapublications.org.

- According to the *New York Times*, approximately **20 percent** of children with ADHD have tried some form of herbal therapy.

- In a 2007 issue of *School Psychology Review*, researchers revealed the results of a 5-year study of 135 preschool students with ADHD symptoms and reported that after using a number of nonmedication intervention strategies, teachers saw a **28 percent** improvement in children's aggression and social skills.

Does Society Need to Change the Way It Approaches ADHD?

66Well-intentioned but misinformed teachers, parents using the Internet to diagnose their children, and hurried doctors are all part of a complex medical system that drives the current practice of misdiagnosing and overmedicating children.99

—Elizabeth J. Roberts, "A Rush to Medicate Young Minds."

66Great strides have been made in the understanding and management of this disorder. Children with AD/HD who would have gone unrecognized and untreated only a few short years ago are now being helped.99

—National Resource Center on AD/HD, "Complementary and Alternative Treatments for AD/HD."

One of the most controversial aspects of ADHD is whether society needs to change the way it approaches the diagnosis and treatment of this disorder.

Attitudes Among Doctors

Some people believe that doctors incorrectly approach the diagnosis and treatment of ADHD. Critics charge that many doctors diagnose the disorder and prescribe medication on the basis of a quick consultation, which does not allow them a thorough knowledge of their patients.

This means that many people, particularly youth, may be misdiagnosed or unnecessarily taking medication. Researchers stress that to properly diagnose ADHD, a psychiatrist should observe a patient for at least a few hours. Yet this recommendation is often ignored. Says psychiatrist Elizabeth J. Roberts, "Today some of my colleagues in psychiatry brag that they can make an initial assessment of a child and write a prescription in less than 20 minutes. Some parents tell me it took their pediatrician only five minutes. Who's the winner in this race?"[68] In an October 2006 study reported in the *Journal for Specialists in Pediatric Nursing*, Julie B. Meaux et al. interviewed 15 college students about their experiences with ADHD medication. The researchers found that after an initial consultation and prescription for a stimulant, the participants usually had no ongoing monitoring or education from their doctor.

> "Critics charge that many doctors diagnose the disorder and prescribe medication on the basis of a quick consultation."

Others contend that the charge that doctors are irresponsible in their diagnoses of ADHD is unfounded. Larry B. Silver, child and adolescent psychiatrist, says, "Studies conducted by the American Medical Association and the Centers for Disease Control and Prevention show that we are not overdiagnosing ADHD. Some parents might have a 'war story' about a physician who diagnoses ADHD in every patient he or she sees, but national surveys do not support this view."[69] In his opinion the increased rate of diagnosis is due to increased education about the disorder among parents and teachers, and also because professionals have learned how to diagnose ADHD more accurately.

The Role of Parents

Some critics believe that the real problem is not ADHD but parenting. They argue that many cases of ADHD are really just cases of problematic behavior due to poor parenting. Writer Gerald K. McOscar asks, "What if at times ADHD is less about hyperactive children than about parents unwilling or unable to cope with the (admittedly challenging) demands and responsibilities of parenthood?"[70] McOscar and others insist that the prevalence of ADHD and the problems that come with it could be reduced by improved parenting. Some people argue that instead of working on their parenting skills, however, many parents turn to an ADHD diagnosis and medication to solve behavior problems in their children. Roberts maintains that many parents actively seek ADHD medication as an easy way to stop their children's difficult behavior. She says, "These days parents cruise the Internet, take self-administered surveys, diagnose their children and choose a medication before they ever set foot in the psychiatrist's office. If the first doctor doesn't prescribe what you want, the next one will."[71]

In response to parenting critiques, many experts maintain that parents should not feel responsible if their children are diagnosed with ADHD. They insist that ADHD is a real medical problem, not something caused by bad parenting. Says E. Clarke Ross, chief executive officer of the organization Children and Adults with Attention-Deficit/Hyperactivity Disorder, "[There is a] mountain of evidence in recent years from government and academic researchers that shows that AD/HD is a real neurological disorder that can have devastating consequences if left untreated."[72]

> " [Some people believe that] the increased rate of diagnosis is due to increased education about the disorder. "

The Role of Teachers

In many cases, teachers are the first ones to suggest that a child be evaluated for ADHD. This is because the symptoms of the disorder, such as hyperactivity and difficulty focusing, are often noticed by teachers because they cause problems in the classroom environment. Whether teachers' help in the diagnosis of ADHD reduces its impact or makes the problem worse is debated. Some people believe that the trend of teachers helping to diagnose ADHD benefits society. They argue that when teachers suggest ADHD, they are helping youth, who might otherwise not be noticed, get the treatment they need. Others fear that many teachers help diagnose ADHD in children because it makes their classrooms easier to control and their test scores higher. According to researcher Helen Schneider, states with higher accountability laws for schools tend to have higher ADHD rates. She explains, "Faced with accountability pressures, teachers are more likely to suggest medical solutions to problems of disruptive behavior and poor academic performance."[73] Greg Norton, a teacher with 18 years of experience teaching special education, is one person who believes that teachers should not diagnose ADHD because they are not qualified to do so. He says, "It irritates me when I see teachers with no formal medical training labeling children with something classified as a 'mental disorder.'"[74] Norton and others believe that this trend leads to harmful overdiagnosis of the disorder.

ADHD Medication Is Overprescribed

Many critics charge that ADHD is overdiagnosed and overmedicated in the United States and elsewhere. In its 2006 report, the International Narcotics Control Board discusses methylphenidate, also called Ritalin, one of the most popular ADHD medications. It finds, "The use of methylphenidate for medical purposes increased significantly in the period 2002–2005. Global calculated consumption of the substance increased from 18.5 tons in 2001 to 30.4 tons in 2005."[75] According to this report, the largest consumption of the drug occurs in the United States, but significant increases have also occurred in other countries, particularly Canada, Israel, and Norway. Many people believe this increase is the result of too many people being diagnosed with ADHD and medication being given to people who do not really need it. However, others contend that the increase in ADHD medication is not due to overprescription but to increased awareness of the disorder. Says Silver, "We are not overprescribing methylphenidate (Ritalin). More individuals of all ages are being given the diagnosis of ADHD."[76]

> " Many experts . . . insist that ADHD is a real medical problem, not something caused by bad parenting. "

Critics of increasing use of ADHD medication charge that its widespread use has also led to widespread abuse of that medication. In 2006 congressional testimony, director of the National Institute on Drug

Abuse Nora D. Volkow explains: "The fact that doctors are prescribing these drugs legitimately and with increasing frequency to treat a variety of ailments leads to the misguided and dangerous conclusion that their non-medical use should be equally safe."[77]

ADHD Medication Is Underprescribed

While some people fear the harms of overprescription of ADHD medication, others point out that in fact, many people who need the medication do not receive it. A number of studies show that many people with ADHD do not take medication. According to a 2003 national study by the Centers for Disease Control and Prevention, of children 17 years old and younger, 56.3 percent with reported ADHD diagnoses are being treated with medication. In a July 2006 article in the *Journal of the American Academy of Child and Adolescent Psychiatry*, Wendy Reich, Hongyan Huang, and Richard D. Todd report the results of their study of ADHD medication use. Despite widespread argument that children are overmedicated for ADHD, Todd says, "What we found was somewhat surprising." He adds, "Only about 58 percent of boys and about 45 percent of girls who had a diagnosis of full-scale ADHD got any medication at all."[78] These researchers believe such a trend has a harmful impact on youth. According to Todd, most of the parents of the children in the study said that their children improved when they started taking medication. Research shows that affluent white boys are most likely to take ADHD medication. Prescription rates are significantly lower among females and lower-income and minority groups.

> " In many cases, teachers are the first ones to suggest that a child be evaluated for ADHD. "

Advertising ADHD Medication

In the United States ADHD medication is advertised to the public, causing protest among many critics. The United States is one of 159 countries that have agreed to a United Nations treaty banning consumer-targeting of psychotropic medications, which includes ADHD medication. However, companies started to advertise ADHD medications in 2001, defending their actions as protected by the First Amendment (this has not been tested in court). According to journalist Karin Klein in a 2007 article in the *Los Angeles Times*, "The results are dramatic. Doctors and therapists increasingly see parents seeking to change their child's medication or coming in with their own diagnosis of ADHD and suggestions for medications they have seen advertised. Many of the companies offer coupons for a free trial supply."[79] Klein says that the United States is the only country to violate the UN treaty, and it also consumes about 85 percent of the stimulants that are manufactured for ADHD.

> **Many critics charge that ADHD is overdiagnosed and overmedicated in the United States and elsewhere.**

She believes that consumer-targeting advertising of ADHD medications is a major cause of this consumption, and she is opposed to such marketing. She says, "Powerful psychotropic medications should be an option of last resort and uninfluenced deliberation, not another brand-name product to add to the back-to-school shopping list."[80] Many critics charge that pharmaceutical companies also have a huge impact on ADHD policy and scientific debate. Researchers Sami Timimi and Nick Radcliffe assert, "Indeed, some argue that ADHD has been conceived and promoted by the pharmaceutical industry in order for there to be an entity for which stimulants could be prescribed."[81] In its 2006 report, the International Narcotics Control Board urged the U.S. government to prohibit public advertisement of stimulants.

Abuse of ADHD Drugs

The abuse of ADHD medication is significant and increasing, primarily among high school– and college-age youth. This abuse is becoming increasingly harmful, they believe, and society should attempt to curb it. In 2006 congressional testimony Volkow says, "These trends in adolescent [prescription drug abuse] are particularly problematic because adolescence is the period of greatest risk . . . for developing addiction. Also, at this stage the brain is still developing and exposure to drugs could interfere with these developmental changes."[82] ADHD medication taken without a prescription is correlated with an increasing number of emergency department visits. In a 2006 report the Substance Abuse and Mental Health Services Administration (SAMHSA) estimates that in 2004, of the visits to the emergency department involving stimulants, 48 percent were for nonmedical use (without a prescription). This non-medical use was most common among people aged 18 to 25. SAMHSA also reports a 108 percent increase in emergency department visits for methylphenidate (marketed as Ritalin and Concerta) between 2004 and 2005. According to a 2008 report by the agency, abuse of ADHD medi-cation is also correlated with a greater likelihood of delinquent behavior. It reports that of youth who engage in nonmedical use of stimulants, over 71 percent of these engage in delinquent behavior, compared with 34 percent of those who do not use stimulants without a prescription.

In a 2004 article the *British Journal of Psychiatry* states, "Attention-deficit hyperactivity disorder (ADHD) has received considerable atten-tion and is a problem that is rarely out of the news. . . . Despite all the research it has been difficult to gain and maintain professional agreement on what ADHD is or what should be done about it."[83] Disagreement over society's approach to ADHD includes opinions on attitudes among doctors, the role of parents and teachers, whether ADHD medication is underprescribed or overprescribed, advertising of ADHD medication, and abuse of ADHD drugs.

Does Society Need to Change the Way It Approaches ADHD?

66 **Physicians and psychologists are supposed to rule out every other disorder or problem that might disrupt attention before making the diagnosis. Yet most children are given the diagnosis after a 15-minute appointment with the pediatrician and a behavior rating scale.** 99

—Nadia Webb and Antara Dietrich, "Gifted and Learning Disabled: A Neuropsychologist's Perspective," *Gifted Education Communicator*, Fall/Winter 2005. www.cagifted.org.

Webb is a practicing neuropsychologist and college professor and is on the board of directors for the organization Supporting Emotional Needs of the Gifted (SENG).

....

66 **Medical . . . awareness of the problem of ADHD has grown considerably so that people, who were underdiagnosed in the past, are being identified and treated.** 99

—Richard K. Nakamura, "Attention Deficit/Hyperactivity Disorders: Are Children Being Overmedicated?" Testimony before the Committee on Government Reform, United States House of Representatives, September 26, 2002. www.nimh.nih.gov.

Nakamura is former director of the National Institute of Mental Health.

....

* Editor's Note: While the definition of a primary source can be narrowly or broadly defined, for the purposes of Compact Research, a primary source consists of: 1) results of original research presented by an organization or researcher; 2) eyewitness accounts of events, personal experience, or work experience; 3) first-person editorials offering pundits' opinions; 4) government officials presenting political plans and/or policies; 5) representatives of organizations presenting testimony or policy.

66 There are, of course, some children who genuinely need pharmaceutical intervention. However, more often than not, this so-called disorder is really the result of combining excessively spirited children with criminally sub-standard parenting skills. 99

—Laura J. Snook, "High on Life: The Biggest Health Care Fraud in History?" *UK MSN*, November 13, 2007. http://uk.msn.com.

Snook is the United Kingdom news editor for Web site *MSN*.

66 Public perceptions of attention-deficit hyperactivity disorder (AD/HD) are replete with myths. . . . Critics often claim that children are needlessly medicated by parents who have not properly managed their unruly, unmotivated or underachieving children. 99

—Phyllis Anne Teeter Ellison, "AD/HD Myths," *Attention!* June 2003.

Ellison is chair of the editorial advisory board and a member of the executive committee for Children and Adults with Attention Deficit/Hyperactivity Disorder (CHADD).

66 Teacher referrals have become a significant factor in determining whether a child will be diagnosed with the disorder. . . . [However] this study suggested that teachers . . . have limited knowledge about ADHD and its treatment with stimulant drug medication. 99

—Vicki E. Snider, Tracey Busch, and Linda Arrowood, "ADHD Teacher Knowledge of Stimulant Medication and ADHD," *LD Online*, 2003. www.ldonline.org.

Snider is coordinator of the Program in Learning Disabilities at the University of Wisconsin–Eau Claire. Busch is a teacher at Audubon Technology and Communication Center in Milwaukee, Wisconsin, and Arrowood is an instructor at the University of Wisconsin–Eau Claire.

66 **Large numbers of children who do have ADHD are going undiagnosed.** 99

—*New Scientist*, "Hyperactivity Drugs Are Out of Control: Some Children Are Misdiagnosed with ADHD, Others Go Undiagnosed. Both May Face Serious Problems," April 1, 2006.

New Scientist is a print and online magazine that provides science and technology news from around the world.

66 **The fact that ADHD is clearly overdiagnosed in some communities and among some groups of children . . . is lost in nationwide estimates of ADHD drug treatment. . . . It is appropriate to be judicious in our use of psychotropic medications and cautious about dismissal of concern about ADHD overdiagnosis.** 99

—Gretchen B. LeFever, Andrea P. Arcona, and David O. Antonuccio, "ADHD Among American Schoolchildren: Evidence of Overdiagnosis and Overuse of Medication," *Scientific Review of Mental Health Practice*, Spring/Summer 2003. www.srmhp.org.

LeFever and Arcona are researchers at the Center for Pediatric Research at the Eastern Virginia Medical School and Children's Hospital of the King's Daughters. Antonuccio is affiliated with the University of Nevada School of Medicine.

66 **Twenty years ago, in our practice of eighteen thousand patients, we had two children who had been diagnosed as *hyperactive*. . . . We now have not two but *thirty-eight* children on Ritalin, Concerta or Strattera. . . . A nineteen-fold increase . . . in twenty years.** 99

—John Crippen, "Suffer the Little Children . . . " *NHS Blog Doctor*, December 21, 2005. http://nhsblogdoc.blogspot.com.

Crippen is a medical doctor and writes a weekly blog about medically related news in the United Kingdom.

66 In promoting their products the pharmaceutical industry funds important research. In promoting their products, the pharmaceutical industry brings important knowledge to professionals and in the case of ADHD to the general public. 99

—Sam Goldstein, "The Marketing of ADHD: Public Service, Corporate Greed, or Business as Usual?" *SamGoldstein.com*, January 2004. www.samgoldstein.com.

Goldstein is a psychologist, an affiliate research professor, editor in chief of the *Journal of Attention Disorders*, and contributing editor to *Attention Magazine*.

66 While advertisements can inform parents of treatment options and raise awareness about the disorder, marketing tends to drive up parental demands for specific drugs regardless of whether they are the best treatment option for a particular child afflicted with the disorder. 99

—Shane Wong, "Storm in a Western Pill—Fear and Empowerment in ADHD Drug Treatment," *ADHD Information Library*, 2007. http://newideas.net.

Wong is editor in chief for *Juxtaposition Global Health Magazine*, a student-run publication based at the University of Toronto.

66 The [International Narcotics Control] Board urges the Government of the United States to prohibit public advertisement of psychotropic substances, including stimulants . . . used for the treatment of ADD. 99

—International Narcotics Control Board, *Report of the International Narcotics Control Board for 2006*. New York: United Nations, 2007.

The International Narcotics Control Board is an independent board that implements the drug conventions of the United Nations.

66 We must immediately address this new Ritalin abuse epidemic in our teens and young adults with much tighter controls on prescription and diversion to this population. 99

—Lawrence Diller, statement to the FDA, March 22, 2006. www.docdiller.com.

Diller practices behavioral pediatrics in Walnut Creek, California, and is author of *Running on Ritalin, Should I Medicate My Child?* and *The Last Normal Child.*

66 Trends in adolescent [prescription drug abuse] are particularly problematic because adolescence is the period of greatest risk . . . for developing addiction. Also, at this stage the brain is still developing and exposure to drugs could interfere with these developmental changes. 99

—Nora D. Volkow, "Efforts of the National Institute on Drug Abuse to Prevent and Treat Prescription Drug Abuse," testimony before the Subcommittee on Criminal Justice, Drug Policy, and Human Resources, Committee on Government Reform, United States House of Representatives, July 26, 2006. www.nida.nih.gov.

Volkow is director of the U.S. National Institute on Drug Abuse.

Facts and Illustrations

Does Society Need to Change
the Way It Approaches ADHD?

- According to a 2007 article in *Pediatrics for Parents*, in only **14.4 percent** of ADHD cases is the diagnosis first suggested by a primary care physician or mental health professional.

- In a 2003 sample of 400 teachers by Vicki E. Snider, Tracey Busch, and Linda Arrowood, only **6 percent** were aware of the lack of definitive evidence about the long-term impact of stimulants on academic achievement.

- In a 2008 article in the *Indian Journal of Pediatrics*, researchers reported the results of a study of 119 children referred for disruptive behavior. Agreement between parents and teachers for a diagnosis of ADHD was only **52 percent**.

- The International Narcotics Control Board reports that between 2001 and 2005 the use of stimulants increased by more than **60 percent**.

- In 2006 a team of researchers at Washington University School of Medicine in St. Louis reported that almost **50 percent** of the children who might benefit from ADHD medication are not receiving it.

Teachers Know Little About ADHD Treatments

The results of a random sample of 200 teachers and 200 special education teachers from Wisconsin is presented in this chart. It shows the percentage of teachers that correctly answered questions about various aspects of stimulant use and ADHD. Many teachers do not thoroughly understand the disorder and its treatment in youth.

True/False Question	Percentage Correct
Short-tern studies show that stimulant medication improves the behaviors associated with ADHD. (True)	86
The long-term side effects of stimulant medications are well understood. (False)	71
Stress and conflict in the student's home life can cause ADHD symptoms. (True)	67
ADHD is the most commonly diagnosed psychiatric disorder of childhood. (True)	58
Over time, stimulant medication loses its effectiveness. (True)	46
Adderall, Ritalin, and Dexedrine have abuse potential similar to Demerol, cocaine, and morphine. (True)	46
Diagnosis of ADHD can be confirmed if stimulant medication improves the child's attention. (False)	33
While on stimulant medication, students exhibit similar amounts of problem behaviors as their normally developing peers. (False)	27
There are data to indicate that ADHD is caused by a brain malfunction. (False)	10
Studies show that stimulant medication has a positive effect on academic achievement in the long run. (False)	6

Source: Vicki E. Snider, Tracey Busch, and Linda Arrowood, "ADHD Teacher Knowledge of Stimulant Medication and ADHD," *LD Online*, 2003. www.ldonline.org.

Approximately 50 Percent of U.S. Children with ADHD Are Taking Medication

These graphs reveal that approximately 50 percent of those youth diagnosed with ADHD are taking medication to treat the disorder. In addition, both diagnosis and medication rates are higher among males than females.

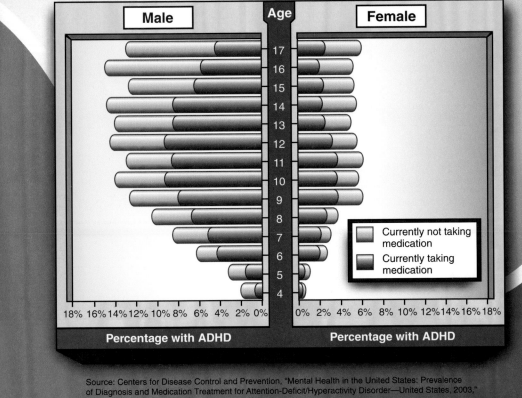

Source: Centers for Disease Control and Prevention, "Mental Health in the United States: Prevalence of Diagnosis and Medication Treatment for Attention-Deficit/Hyperactivity Disorder—United States, 2003," *MMWR Weekly*, September 2, 2005. www.cdc.gov.

- According to a report from pharmacy benefits manager Medco Health Solutions Inc., use of ADHD medication increased almost **19 percent** among ages 20 to 44 in 2005 and decreased **5 percent** in children under 10.

- According to pharmaceutical information and consulting firm IMS Health, spending on ADHD drugs increased from **$759 million** in 2000 to **$3.1 billion** in 2004.

Nonmedical Stimulant Use Correlated with Delinquent Behaviors

The majority of U.S. stimulant prescriptions are for ADHD; however, many people also use stimulants without a prescription. According to this graph, the percentage of youth aged 12 to 17 who engaged in various delinquent behaviors in 2005 and 2006 was significantly higher among those who used stimulants without a prescription.

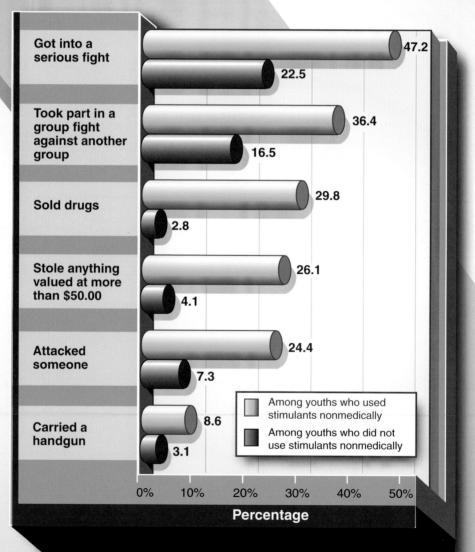

Got into a serious fight: 47.2 / 22.5

Took part in a group fight against another group: 36.4 / 16.5

Sold drugs: 29.8 / 2.8

Stole anything valued at more than $50.00: 26.1 / 4.1

Attacked someone: 24.4 / 7.3

Carried a handgun: 8.6 / 3.1

Among youths who used stimulants nonmedically
Among youths who did not use stimulants nonmedically

Percentage

Source: Substance Abuse and Mental Health Services Administration, "Nonmedical Stimulant Use, Other Drug Use, Delinquent Behaviors, and Depression Among Adolescents," *The NSDUH Report*, February 28, 2008. http://oas.samhsa.gov.

Ritalin Abuse Commonly Researched Online

This graph shows estimates of a number of Ritalin-related searches on Internet search engines for a one-year period. Many of these top 30 search combinations are related to Ritalin abuse, indicating that such abuse is prevalent.

Search Terms	Number of Searches
Buy Ritalin	51,477
Ritalin online	23,547
Ritalin abuse	13,671
Buy Ritalin online	10,992
Ritalin weight	10,953
Ritalin weight loss	10,951
Ritalin dosage	9,320
Ritalin no prescription	8,996
Smoking Ritalin	8,396
Ritalin LA	8,164
Ritalin without a prescription	8,128
Snorting Ritalin	7,948
Ritalin cocaine	6,570
History of Ritalin	5,482
Ritalin use in schools	5,475
Buying Ritalin	4,747
Brain effects of Ritalin	4,745
Ritalin for children	4,470
Side effects of Ritalin	4,275
Alternatives to Ritalin	3,770
Ritalin patch	3,650
Ritalin adults	3,395
Ritain for adults	3,291
Substitute for Ritalin	3,287
Herbal substitute for Ritalin	3,285
Ritalin drug	3,158
Pictures of Ritalin	2,920
Ritalin snorting	2,745
Ritalin vs Adderall	2,446
What is Ritalin?	2,269

Source: Clear Haven Center, "Ritalin Addictions—'Kiddie Cocaine' Gaining Popularity," 2007. www.clearhavencenter.com.

Key People and Advocacy Groups

Thomas Armstrong: Armstrong is the author of numerous books and articles about ADHD, including *The Myth of the A.D.D. Child*.

Attention Deficit Disorder Association (ADDA): ADDA is an international organization that works to provide information, resources, and networking to adults and youth with ADHD.

Russell A. Barkley: Barkley is an internationally recognized authority on ADHD. He has received numerous awards over his career for his work in ADHD and the field of psychology.

Children and Adults with Attention Deficit/Hyperactivity Disorder (CHADD): CHADD is a national nonprofit organization that provides education, advocacy, and support for children and adults with ADHD.

Lawrence Diller: Diller is a pediatrician in Walnut Creek, California, and author of *Running on Ritalin: A Physician Reflects on Children, Society and Performance in a Pill*. He is opposed to medicating children for ADHD.

Edward M. Hallowell: Hallowell is an internationally recognized ADHD expert and founder of the Hallowell Center for Emotional and Cognitive Health. He is coauthor of the ADHD book *Driven to Distraction* as well as *Answers to Distraction* and *Delivered from Distraction*.

Judith Rapoport: Rapoport is chief of the child psychology branch at the National Institute of Mental Health where she investigates the causes and treatment of psychiatric disorders, including ADHD, in children.

Eric Taylor: Taylor is a child neuropsychiatrist at the Institute of Psychiatry at King's College, London. He is the author of *People with Hyperactivity: Understanding and Managing Their Problems* and of numerous scientific papers on ADHD.

Sami Timimi: Timimi is a child and adolescent psychiatrist and author of *Pathological Child Psychiatry and the Medicalization of Childhood.* He believes that ADHD is a cultural construct.

Nora Volkow: Volkow is director of the U.S. National Institute on Drug Abuse. Her research on ADHD and the brain has been important in increasing knowledge about how the brains of people with ADHD differ from those without the disorder.

Chronology

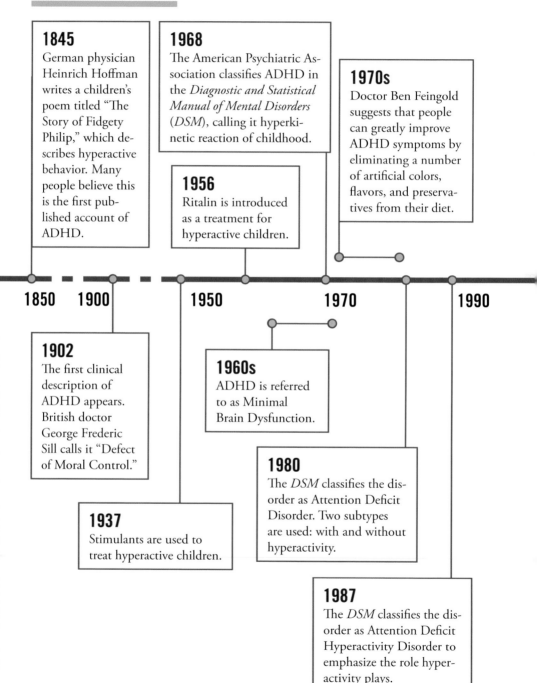

1845
German physician Heinrich Hoffman writes a children's poem titled "The Story of Fidgety Philip," which describes hyperactive behavior. Many people believe this is the first published account of ADHD.

1968
The American Psychiatric Association classifies ADHD in the *Diagnostic and Statistical Manual of Mental Disorders* (*DSM*), calling it hyperkinetic reaction of childhood.

1970s
Doctor Ben Feingold suggests that people can greatly improve ADHD symptoms by eliminating a number of artificial colors, flavors, and preservatives from their diet.

1956
Ritalin is introduced as a treatment for hyperactive children.

1850   1900   1950   1970   1990

1902
The first clinical description of ADHD appears. British doctor George Frederic Sill calls it "Defect of Moral Control."

1960s
ADHD is referred to as Minimal Brain Dysfunction.

1980
The *DSM* classifies the disorder as Attention Deficit Disorder. Two subtypes are used: with and without hyperactivity.

1937
Stimulants are used to treat hyperactive children.

1987
The *DSM* classifies the disorder as Attention Deficit Hyperactivity Disorder to emphasize the role hyperactivity plays.

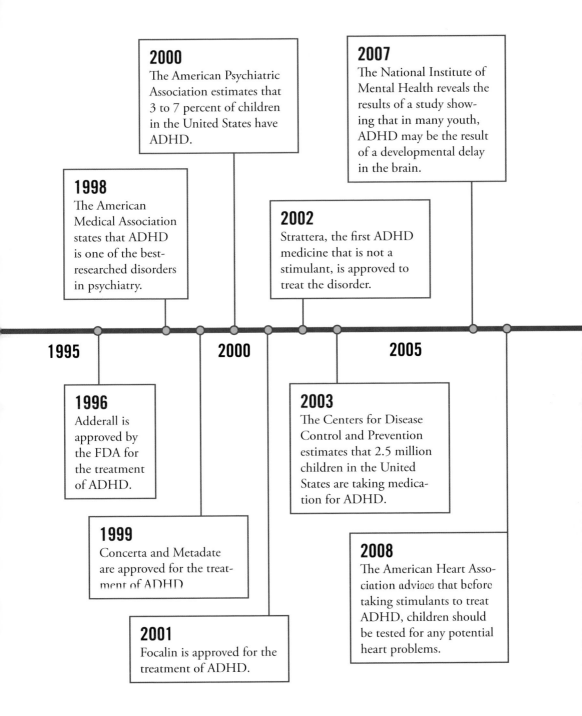

2000
The American Psychiatric Association estimates that 3 to 7 percent of children in the United States have ADHD.

2007
The National Institute of Mental Health reveals the results of a study showing that in many youth, ADHD may be the result of a developmental delay in the brain.

1998
The American Medical Association states that ADHD is one of the best-researched disorders in psychiatry.

2002
Strattera, the first ADHD medicine that is not a stimulant, is approved to treat the disorder.

1995

2000

2005

1996
Adderall is approved by the FDA for the treatment of ADHD.

2003
The Centers for Disease Control and Prevention estimates that 2.5 million children in the United States are taking medication for ADHD.

1999
Concerta and Metadate are approved for the treatment of ADHD.

2008
The American Heart Association advises that before taking stimulants to treat ADHD, children should be tested for any potential heart problems.

2001
Focalin is approved for the treatment of ADHD.

Related Organizations

American Academy of Child & Adolescent Psychiatry (AACAP)

3615 Wisconsin Ave. NW

Washington, DC 20016

phone: (202) 966-7300 • fax: (202) 966-2891

Web site: www.aacap.org

AACAP is the leading national professional medical association dedicated to treating and improving the quality of life for children, adolescents, and families affected by mental, behavioral, or developmental disorders, including ADHD. It is a membership-based organization, composed of over 7,500 child and adolescent psychiatrists and other physicians. AACAP distributes information in an effort to promote an understanding of mental illnesses and to remove the stigma associated with them, advance efforts in prevention of mental illnesses, and assure proper treatment and access to services for children and adolescents.

American Psychological Association (APA)

750 First St. NE

Washington, DC 20002

phone: (800) 374-2721

Web site: www.apa.org

The American Psychological Association is a scientific and professional organization that represents psychology in the United States. It works to promote the health, education, and public welfare of Americans. The APA's Web site provides information and education about ADHD.

Attention Deficit Disorder Association (ADDA)

15000 Commerce Parkway, Suite C

Mount Laurel, NJ 08054

phone: (856) 439-9099 • fax: (856) 439-0525

e-mail: adda@add.org • Web site: www.add.org

The Attention Deficit Disorder Association is an international organization that works to provide information, resources, and networking to adults and young adults with ADHD and to those professionals who work with them. ADDA provides information about ADHD treatments and strategies for helping those with ADHD lead better lives.

Attention Deficit Disorder Resources

223 Tacoma Ave. S., #100

Tacoma, WA 98402

phone: (253) 759-5085 • fax: (253) 572-3700

Web site: www.addresources.org

Founded in 1993, Attention Deficit Disorder Resources is a nonprofit organization dedicated to supporting and educating people with ADHD and those who interact with them in the community. The organization's Web site has articles about ADHD and links to other ADHD-related Web sites.

Children and Adults with Attention Deficit/Hyperactivity Disorder (CHADD)

8181 Professional Pl., Suite 150

Landover, MD 20785

phone: (301) 306-7070 • fax: (301) 306-7090

Web site: www.chadd.org

CHADD is a national nonprofit organization that provides education, advocacy, and support for children and adults with ADHD. It was founded in 1987 and has over 16,000 members in 200 local chapters throughout the United States. It provides a wide variety of ADHD information both in print and on its Web site.

Mental Health America

2000 N. Beauregard St., 6th Floor

Alexandria, VA 22311

phone (703) 684-7722 • fax (703) 684-5968

Web site: www.nmha.org

Mental Health America is a nonprofit organization dedicated to helping all people live mentally healthier lives. It works to help people understand how to protect and improve their mental health and when to look for help for themselves or friends or family members. MHA's Web site contains numerous fact sheets on ADHD.

National Alliance Against Mandated Mental Health Screening & Psychiatric Drugging of Children

e-mail: RitalinDeath@gmail.com • Web site: www.RitalinDeath.com

The National Alliance Against Mandated Mental Health Screening & Psychiatric Drugging of Children is an organization opposed to the use of ADHD drugs by children. It believes that many children are incorrectly diagnosed with ADHD when they actually have other health problems or learning disorders. Its Web site contains information about the harms of Ritalin and other ADHD medications.

National Alliance on Mental Illness (NAMI)

Colonial Place Three

2107 Wilson Blvd., Suite 300

Arlington, VA 22201

phone: (703) 524-7600 • fax: (703) 524-9094

e-mail: info@nami.org • Web site: www.nami.org

NAMI is an organization dedicated to eradicating mental illness and improving the quality of life for all people affected by mental illness. It provides support, education, and advocacy for those affected by ADHD. Its Web site provides research and fact sheets about ADHD and the medication used to treat it.

National Center for Girls and Women with AD/HD

3268 Arcadia Pl. NW

Washington, DC 20015

phone: (888) 238-8588 • fax: (202) 966-1561

e-mail: contact@ncgiadd.org • Web site: www.ncgiadd.org

The National Center for Girls and Women with AD/HD aims to raise awareness of the impact of ADHD on women and girls. It also promotes research on ADHD in females and works to disseminate information about ADHD to families, medical and mental health professionals, educators, and the media.

National Institute of Mental Health (NIMH)

Science Writing, Press, and Dissemination Branch

6001 Executive Blvd., Room 8184, MSC 9663

Bethesda, MD 20892

phone: (301) 443-4513 • fax: (301) 443-4279

e-mail: nimhinfo@nih.gov • Web site: www.nimh.nih.gov

The National Institute of Mental Health is dedicated to research that will reduce the burden of mental illness and behavioral disorders, including ADHD. Its Web site contains fact sheets, overviews, and recent research updates on the disorder.

For Further Research

Books

Russell A. Barkley, Kevin R. Murphy, and Mariellen Fischer, *ADHD in Adults: What the Science Says.* New York: Guilford, 2008.

Thomas Brown, *Attention Deficit Disorder: The Unfocused Mind in Children and Adults.* New Haven, CT: Yale University Press, 2006.

Brian B. Doyle, *Understanding and Treating Adults with Attention Deficit Hyperactivity Disorder.* Washington, DC: American Psychiatric, 2006.

Mina K. Dulcan, ed., *Helping Parents, Youth, and Teachers Understand Medications for Behavioral and Emotional Problems.* Washington, DC: American Psychiatric, 2007.

Robert Jergen, *The Little Monster: Growing Up with ADHD.* Lanham, MD: ScarecrowEducation, 2004.

Michelle P. Larimer, ed., *Attention Deficit Hyperactivity Disorder (ADHD) Research.* New York: Nova Medical, 2005.

Vincent J. Monastra, *Parenting Children with ADHD: 10 Lessons That Medicine Cannot Teach.* Washington, DC: American Psychological Association, 2005.

Annette U. Rickel and Ronald T. Brown, *Attention-Deficit/Hyperactivity Disorder in Children and Adults.* Cambridge, MA: Hogrefe & Huber, 2007.

Mark Selikowitz, *ADHD: The Facts.* Oxford: Oxford University Press, 2004.

Larry B. Silver, *Attention-Deficit/Hyperactivity Disorder.* Washington, DC: American Psychiatric, 2004.

Eric Taylor, ed., *People with Hyperactivity: Understanding and Managing Their Problems.* London: Mac Keith, 2007.

Periodicals

Consumers Union, "Consumer Reports Best Buy Drugs: Evaluating Prescription Drugs Used to Treat Attention Deficit Hyperactivity Disorder; Comparing Effectiveness, Safety, and Price," 2005.

D. Daley, "Attention Deficit Hyperactivity Disorder: A Review of the Essential Facts," *Child: Care, Health & Development*, March 2006.

Economist, "Desperate Parents, Dangerous Drugs, Hyperactive Children," April 22, 2006.

Joel Garreau, "A Dose of Genius; 'Smart Pills' Are on the Rise. But Is Taking Them Wise?" *Washington Post*, June 11, 2006.

Edward M. Hallowell, "ADD's Black Box Scare," *Los Angeles Times*, February 26, 2006.

Melissa Healy, "The Push to Label; When Kids Have Behavioral Problems, Diagnoses and Drugs Often Follow. Has Psychiatry Gone Overboard on Medicating Children?" *Los Angeles Times*, November 5, 2007.

———, "The Ritalin Kids Grow Up; on Their Terms; Now Adults, Many in the 'ADD Generation' Are Saying No to Their Meds," *Los Angeles Times*, December 18, 2006.

Matt Isaacs, "No Quick Fix," *Diablo Magazine*, March 2008.

Karin Klein, "Pencils, Pens, Meds," *Los Angeles Times*, August 20, 2007.

Donna Leinward, "Prescription Drugs Find Place in Teen Culture," *USA Today*, June 13, 2006.

Donna McCann et al., "Food Additives and Hyperactive Behavior in 3-Year-Old and 8/9-Year-Old Children in the Community: A Randomised Double-Blinded, Placebo-Controlled Study," *Lancet*, September 6, 2007.

Julie B. Meaux et al., "Stimulant Medications: A Trade-Off? The Lived Experiences of Adolescents with ADHD," *Journal for Specialists in Pediatric Nursing*, October 2006.

Lindsay Minnema, "Will Kids Outgrow ADHD? Experts Help Parents Put Findings in Perspective, *Washington Post*, November 27, 2007.

New Scientist, "Attention Please: The Way We Deal with Hyperactivity Disorder Leaves a Lot to Be Desired," April 1, 2006.

———, "Hyperactivity Drugs Are Out of Control: Some Children Are Misdiagnosed with ADHD, Others Go Undiagnosed. Both Face Serious Problems," April 1, 2006.

Elizabeth J. Roberts, "A Rush to Medicate Young Minds," *Washington Post*, October 8, 2006.

Helen Schneider, "My Child and ADHD: Chances of Being Diagnosed," *Pediatrics for Parents*, September 2007.

Sue Shellenbarger, "The Creative Energy Behind ADHD," *Wall Street Journal*, April 17, 2008.

Nancy Shute, "ADHD Brains Might Need More Growing Time," *U.S. News & World Report*, November 12, 2007.

Sami Timimi and Eric Taylor, "ADHD Is Best Understood as a Cultural Construct," *British Journal of Psychiatry*, no. 184, 2004.

Victoria L. Vetter et al., "Cardiovascular Monitoring of Children and Adolescents with Heart Disease Receiving Stimulant Drugs: A Scientific Statement from the American Heart Association Council on Cardiovascular Disease in the Young Congenital Cardiac Defects Committee and the Council on Cardiovascular Nursing," *Circulation*, April 21, 2008.

Nadia Webb and Antara Dietrich, "Gifted and Learning Disabled: A Neuropsychologist's Perspective," *Gifted Education Communicator*, Fall/Winter 2005.

Ron Winslow, "New Guidelines Urge Heart Tests Before Kids Take ADHD Drugs," *Wall Street Journal*, April 22, 2008.

Internet Sources

Mayo Clinic, "Attention-Deficit/Hyperactivity Disorder (ADHD)," February 16, 2007. www.mayoclinic.com/health/adhd/DS00275.

National Center on Birth Defects and Developmental Disabilities, Centers for Disease Control and Prevention, "What Is Attention-Deficit/Hyperactivity Disorder (ADHD)?" September 20, 2005. www.cdc.gov/ncbddd/adhd/what.htm.

National Institute of Mental Health, "Attention Deficit Hyperactivity Disorder," 2006. www.nimh.nih.gov/health/publications/adhd/summary.shtml.

New York Times, "ADHD In-Depth Report." http://health.nytimes.com/health/guides/disease/attention-deficit-hyperactivity-disorder-adhd/in-depth-report.html.

TeensHealth, "ADHD," February 2006. www.kidshealth.org/PageManager.jsp?dn=KidsHealth&lic=1&article_set=20413&cat_id=20179&.

Source Notes

Overview

1. Quoted in Jim Dryden, "Washington Researchers Find Almost Half of Kids with ADHD Are Not Being Treated," Washington University School of Medicine, August 3, 2006. http://mednews.wustl.edu.

2. Nadia Webb and Antara Dietrich, "Gifted and Learning Disabled: A Neuropsychologist's Perspective," *Gifted Education Communicator*, Fall/Winter 2005. www.cagifted.org.

3. Quoted in Laura J. Snook, "High on Life: The Biggest Health Care Fraud in History?" *UK MSN*, November 13, 2007. http://uk.msn.com.

4. Melissa Healy, "The Push to Label; When Kids Have Behavioral Problems, Diagnoses and Drugs Often Follow. Has Psychiatry Gone Overboard on Medicating Children?" *Los Angeles Times*, November 5, 2007, p. F1.

5. Brian B. Doyle, *Understanding and Treating Adults with Attention Deficit Hyperactivity Disorder*. Washington, DC: American Psychiatric, 2006. p. vii.

6. American Academy of Child and Adolescent Psychiatry, "ADHD—a Guide for Families." www.aacap.org.

7. Doyle, *Understanding and Treating Adults*, p. vii.

8. Quoted in Sue Shellenbarger, "The Creative Energy Behind ADHD," *Wall Street Journal*, April 17, 2008. http://online.wsj.com.

9. Centers for Disease Control and Prevention, "Mental Health in the United States: Prevalence of Diagnosis and Medication Treatment for Attention-Deficit/Hyperactivity Disorder—United States, 2003," September 2, 2005. www.cdc.gov.

10. Consumers Union, "Consumer Reports Best Buy Drugs: Evaluating Prescription Drugs Used to Treat Attention Deficit Hyperactivity Disorder; Comparing Effectiveness, Safety, and Price," *Consumer Reports*, 2005, p. 20.

11. Nora D. Volkow, "Scientific Research on Prescription Drug Abuse," testimony before the Subcommittee on Crime and Drugs, Committee on the Judiciary and the Caucus on International Narcotics Control, United States Senate," March 12, 2008. www.nida.nih.gov.

12. Quoted in Kathleen Doheny, "Treating ADHD: Drugs or Therapy Work," *WebMD*, July 20, 2007. www.webmd.com.

13. Thomas Armstrong, "The Myth of Attention Deficit Disorder," *Dr. Thomas Armstrong*. www.thomasarmstrong.com.

14. Sami Timimi, "ADHD Is Best Understood as a Cultural Construct," *British Journal of Psychiatry*, vol. 184, 2004, pp. 8–9.

15. National Institute of Mental Health, "Attention Deficit Hyperactivity Disorder," 2006. www.nimh.nih.gov.

16. Mental Health America, "Factsheet: AD/HD and Adults," January 9, 2007. www.mentalhealthamerica.net.

17. Eric Taylor, "Clinical and Epidemiological Foundations," in Eric Taylor, ed., *People with Hyperactivity: Understanding and Managing Their Problems*. London: Mac Keith, 2007, p. 11.

18. F. Gonzalez-Lima, "Cortical and Limbic Systems Mediating the Predisposition to Attention Deficit and Hyperactivity," in Michelle P. Larimer, ed., *Attention Deficit Hyperactivity Disorder*

(ADHD) Research. New York: Nova Medical, 2005, p. 2.

19. Quoted in Rick Nauert, "Is ADHD the Leading Childhood Disorder?" *Psych Central*, April 9, 2007. http://psychcentral.com.

20. U.S. Department of Education, "Identifying and Treating Attention Deficit Hyperactivity Disorder: A Resource for Home and School," September 2006. www.edpubs.org.

What Causes ADHD?

21. *ADDitude*, "ADHD: A Biological Disorder." www.additudemag.com.

22. Quoted in Lindsay Minnema, "Will Kids Outgrow ADHD? Experts Help Parents Put Findings in Perspective," *Washington Post*, November 27, 2007, p. F8.

23. Russell A. Barkley, "About ADHD: A Fact Sheet by Dr. Barkley," Russell A. Barkley, Ph.D.: The Official Site. www.russellbarkley.org.

24. Doyle, *Understanding and Treating Adults*, p. 89.

25. Edward M. Hallowell, "Can You Prevent Your Child from Developing ADHD?" *ADDitude*. www.additude mag.com.

26. Gabor Maté, "About the Book," *Scattered*. www.scatteredminds.com.

27. "Happy Girl," "The Feingold Diet: Comments," *ADDitude*, March 20, 2008. www.additudemag.com.

28. National Alliance on Mental Illness, "Attention Deficit/Hyperactivity Disorder," 2008. www.nami.org.

29. D. Daley, "Attention Deficit Hyperactivity Disorder: A Review of the Essential Facts," *Child: Care, Health & Development*, March 2006, p. 196.

30. Maté, "About the Book."

31. National Institute of Mental Health, "Attention Deficit Hyperactivity Disorder."

32. Attention Deficit Disorder Association, "Fact Sheet on Attention Deficit Hyperactivity Disorder (ADHD/ADD)." www.add.org.

33. Larry B. Silver, *Attention-Deficit/Hyperactivity Disorder*. Washington, DC: American Psychiatric, 2004, p. 4.

34. Doyle, *Understanding and Treating Adults*, p. 289.

35. Deborah Merlin, "How Environmental Toxins Affect Student Performance," *Victory over ADHD*. www.victoryoveradhd.com.

36. Sami Timimi and Nick Radcliffe, "The Rise and Rise of ADHD," in Craig Newnes and Nick Radcliffe, eds., *Making and Breaking Children's Lives*. Ross-On-Wye, UK: PCCS Books, 2005, p. 64.

37. Armstrong, "The Myth of Attention Deficit Disorder."

38. Russell A. Barkley et al., "International Consensus Statement on ADHD," *Clinical Child and Family Psychology Review*, June 2002, p. 89.

How Does ADHD Affect a Person's Life?

39. Doyle, *Understanding and Treating Adults*, p. 277.

40. Blythe Grossberg, "Finding Joy on the Job," *ADDitude*. www.additudemag.com.

41. Quoted in Grossberg, "Finding Joy on the Job."

42. *New York Times*, "ADHD In-Depth Report," December 27, 2007. www.nytimes.com.

43. Melinda White, "How Adult ADHD Affects Relationships: Strategies for Coping," *ADD Consults*, October 20, 2004. www.addconsults.com.

44. Mental Health America, "Factsheet: AD/HD and Kids," July 18, 2007. www.mentalhealthamerica.net.

45. Mental Health America, "Factsheet:

AD/HD and Adults," January 9, 2007. www.mentalhealthamerica.net.

46. Taylor, "Clinical and Epidemiological Foundations," p. 16.

47. Steven A. Safren, Carol A. Perlman, Susan Sprich, and Michael W. Otto, *Mastering Your Adult ADHD: A Cognitive-Behavioral Treatment Program.* New York: Oxford University Press, 2005, p. 6.

48. Kurt Robinson, "Common Disorders Associated with ADHD," *Insight Journal*, January 3, 2005. www.insight-journal.com.

49. Jay Giedd, "ADHD and Substance Abuse," *Medscape*, June 3, 2003. www.medscape.com.

50. Rakesh Jain, interviewed by Richard Weisler, "ADHD and Substance Use Disorders: An Expert Interview with Richard Weisler, MD, and Rakesh Jain, MD, MPH," *Medscape*, November 29, 2006. www.medscape.com.

51. *New Scientist*, "Attention Please: The Way We Deal with Hyperactivity Disorder Leaves a Lot to Be Desired," April 1, 2006, p. 5.

52. Edward M. Hallowell, "ADD's Black Box Scare," *Los Angeles Times*, February 26, 2006, p. M5.

53. Barkley et al., "International Consensus Statement on ADHD," p. 89.

How Should ADHD Be Treated?

54. Mayo Clinic, interview with William Barbaresi, "ADHD Medications: Are They Safe?" April 20, 2006. www.mayoclinic.com.

55. Lawrence Weathers, "Stimulant Drugs for ADHD and ADD," *Answers for ADHD Questions*. www.adhdhelp.org.

56. Gerald K. McOscar, "ADHD," *ifeminists.com*, May 24, 2006. www.ifeminists.net.

57. Almut G. Winterstein et al., "Cardiac Safety of Central Nervous System Stimulants in Children and Adolescents with Attention-Deficit/Hyperactivity Disorder," *Pediatrics*, December 2007. http://pediatrics.aappublications.org.

58. Hallowell, "ADD's Black Box Scare," p. M5.

59. Quoted in Lawrence Smith, "Strattera Side Effects," *Death from Ritalin*. www.ritalindeath.com.

60. Consumers Union, "Consumer Reports Best Buy Drugs: Evaluating Prescription Drugs Used to Treat," p. 9.

61. Silver, *Attention-Deficit/Hyperactivity Disorder*, p. 120.

62. Julie B. Meaux et al., "Stimulant Medications: A Trade-Off? The Lived Experiences of Adolescents with ADHD," *Journal for Specialists in Pediatric Nursing*, October 2006, p. 221.

63. Safren, Perlman, Sprich, and Otto, *Mastering Your Adult ADHD*, pp. 4–5.

64. Quoted in Melissa Healy, "The Ritalin Kids Grow Up; On Their Terms; Now Adults, Many in the 'ADD Generation' Are Saying No to Their Meds," *Los Angeles Times*, December 18, 2006. p. F1.

65. Hallowell, "ADD's Black Box Scare," p. M5.

66. National Alliance on Mental Illness, "Attention-Deficit/Hyperactivity Disorder," 2008.

67. Quoted in *Healthy Place*, "New Treatment Alternatives for ADD, ADHD and Other Learning Disabilities," June 16, 2003. www.healthyplace.com.

Does Society Need to Change the Way It Approaches ADHD?

68. Elizabeth J. Roberts, "A Rush to Medicate Young Minds," *Washington Post*, October 8, 2006, p. B7.

69. Silver, *Attention-Deficit/Hyperactivity Disorder*, p. 5.

70. McOscar, "ADHD."

71. Roberts, "A Rush to Medicate Young Minds," p. B7.

72. E. Clarke Ross, "AD/HD Is Real and the Earth Is Round," CHADD Leadership Blog, November 19, 2007. http://chaddleadershipblog.blogspot. com.

73. Helen Schneider, "My Child and ADHD: Chances of Being Diagnosed," *Pediatrics for Parents*, September 2007.

74. Greg Norton, "ADHD Diagnosis," *AllExperts*, March 4, 2006. http:// en.allexperts.com.

75. International Narcotics Control Board, *Report of the International Narcotics Control Board for 2006*. New York: United Nations, 2002, p. 18.

76. Silver, *Attention-Deficit/Hyperactivity Disorder*, p. 5.

77. Nora D. Volkow, "Efforts of the National Institute on Drug Abuse to Prevent and Treat Prescription Drug Abuse," testimony before the Subcommittee on Criminal Justice, Drug Policy, and Human Resources, Committee on Government Reform, United States House of Representatives, July 26, 2006. www.nida.nih.gov.

78. Quoted in Dryden, "Washington Researchers Find."

79. Karin Klein, "Pencils, Pens, Meds," *Los Angeles Times*, August 20, 2007. www.latimes.com.

80. Klein, "Pencils, Pens, Meds."

81. Timimi and Radcliffe, "The Rise and Rise of ADHD," p. 67.

82. Volkow, "Efforts of the National Institute."

83. Mary Cannon, Kwame McKenzie, and Andrew Sims, "ADHD Is Best Understood as a Cultural Construct," *British Journal of Psychiatry*, vol. 184, 2004, p. 8.

List of Illustrations

Index

About the Author

Andrea C. Nakaya, a native of New Zealand, holds a BA in English and an MA in Communication from San Diego State University. She currently lives in Encinitas, California, with her husband Jamie and their two children, Natalie and Shane. In her free time she enjoys traveling, reading, gardening, and snowboarding.